I AM FULL

I AM FULL

STORIES FOR JACOB

Dan Yashinsky

Signature
EDITIONS

Cover design by Doowah Design.
Cover image by Gabi Caruso, photo by Bernard Kelly.

This book was printed on Ancient Forest Friendly paper.
Printed and bound in Canada by Hignell Book Printing Inc.

We acknowledge the support of the Canada Council for the Arts and the Manitoba Arts Council for our publishing program.

Library and Archives Canada Cataloguing in Publication

Title: I am full : stories for Jacob / Dan Yashinsky.
Names: Yashinsky, Dan, author.
Identifiers: Canadiana (print) 20230526276 |
Canadiana (ebook) 20230526284 |
ISBN 9781773241272 (softcover) |
ISBN 9781773241289 (EPUB)
Subjects: LCSH: Yashinsky-Zavitz, Jacob—Fiction. |
LCGFT: Biographical fiction.
Classification: LCC PS8597.A85 I23 2023 |
DDC C818/.54—dc23

Signature Editions
P.O. Box 206, RPO Corydon, Winnipeg, Manitoba, R3M 3S7
www.signature-editions.com

For everyone living with Prader-Willi Syndrome,

and all the people who love them.

"Your son Jacob is not an ordinary person."

— Jacob, age 6, to his parents

Prologue

When our son Jacob was four he met a man at the corner of Vaughan Road and St. Clair Avenue West here in Toronto. The man had a tool belt and coveralls. Jacob looked him up and down, and asked: "What kind of man are you?" The man laughed, and said, "What kind of little boy are you?"

Jacob Evan Yashinsky-Zavitz had a brief twenty-six years to show us and the world what kind of man he was. He was generous, courtly, warm-hearted, compassionate. He had the gift of welcoming everyone, especially those who were, like him, physically and intellectually different. He had formidable patience when it mattered (good for fishing and pearl-knotting), a passion for beauty (good for jewellery-making and photography), a good head for patterns and games (he rarely lost at Scrabble or Settlers of Catan). He was a gifted poet, and an ardent boyfriend—especially if a date included Korean pancakes on Bloor Street, or sushi on St. Clair. He sold his pearl necklaces and earrings at craft shows across the city, schmoozing knowledgably with each customer. He used his hard-earned money to buy the finest fishing gear, and we have countless photos of surprised-looking, soon-to-be-released bass and pike to show how skilled he was on the water. He was the funniest person I've ever known, diving in and through language with exuberance and originality. And he lived his life with enormous courage, dealing every day with the intense, constant, demoralizing hunger—known as hyperphagia—that accompanies Prader-Willi Syndrome (PWS), a genetic condition affecting one in 15,000 people. We had never heard of it until he was diagnosed at the age of four. This is what we learned: According to the Ontario Prader-Willi Syndrome Association, PWS is the most common genetic cause of life-threatening obesity in children. People with Prader-Willi Syndrome have a problem in their hypothalamus, a part of the brain that normally controls feelings of fullness or hunger. As a result, they never feel full and have a constant urge to eat that they cannot control. Most cases of Prader-Willi syndrome result from a spontaneous genetic error in genes on chromosome 15 that occurs at conception. In very rare cases, the mutation is inherited.

Despite the daily challenges of this disability (I think of it as being "dys-labelled" instead of disabled), Jacob's natural wit, sheer heart, and abundance of spirit helped him create, with the love of his family and friends and a circle of great support workers, a beautiful life. When he was six-and-a-half years old, he said to me, "Could you get me paper? I'm going to write about superheroes!" Jacob was and is the closest thing to a superhero I've ever known.

It was July 2, 2018. We were coming back from a great weekend in Montreal. Jacob and his best friend Effie had spent their time taking photos, sipping beers on patios, eating extravagant desserts (a very infrequent experience for someone with PWS), and generally having a wonderful time. My close friend Michael Pestel had come up from Connecticut to perform with me— I'm a storyteller and he's a musician and sculptor—and to enjoy the city. It was the hottest weekend in a hundred years, and our bed-and-breakfast on St. Laurent was broiling. None of us slept much the night before the trip home. Jacob, Effie, and I set out on the drive down the 401 to Toronto. He ate a Cuban sandwich I'd found at a little place in the Plateau neighbourhood where we were staying, and he told me how delicious it was. Then he said, "I am full!"—a very rare statement coming from him—and fell asleep. Effie was dozing in the back seat. The air conditioning wasn't working well, and the car was steamy, and I was glad to see there was a service station a few kilometres ahead. I'd pull over and have a little nap, I thought. I didn't want to open the window or turn on the radio because I didn't want to wake them up. I knew I was tired, but surely I wasn't *that* tired. I was daydreaming about the cottage Jacob and I were planning to go to in two days for our annual fishing expedition. Then I fell asleep. The car ran off the road and flipped in the air. When it stopped turning and bouncing, it was resting with the driver's side down. Effie told me afterwards she felt the spirit of her late father protecting her in the back seat. But Jacob was held in a position where the weight of his body was pressing against his heart. The trauma doctor who treated him when he was airlifted to Ottawa Civic Hospital told us this is what cut off the oxygen to his brain. The people who stopped on the highway to help us called the police, and we could even hear the sirens of the ambulance racing towards us as I held him in my arms and he lost consciousness. They arrived a minute too late. He didn't wake up again. Jacob stayed alive for eight more days, and his mother and brother were able to come to Ottawa to keep a loving vigil, and to tell him how much we loved him, and to finally say goodbye.

We never imagine that we may become, through terminal illness or unspeakable accident, the legacy-bearers for our own children. And then the unimaginable happens and we are still somehow here and our child is gone and all that's left are stories. "A person is not dead unless they have been forgotten," says the old West African proverb. And so we become the storykeepers for our lost beloveds, because who else can be? When Jacob died I sought out other parents who'd lost their sons and daughters. They became my informal bereavement group. Incredibly to me, each mourner somehow found their own way to continue living. And not just living: holding jobs, working to do good in the world, volunteering, making music and art, continuing to love their other children and grandchildren, supporting their partners and community, helping other bereaved parents, keeping the stories of their loved ones alive.

We are all, ultimately, each other's storykeepers. I learned about the value of storykeeping when I worked for five years as the storyteller-in-residence at Baycrest Centre, a geriatric hospital and long-term care centre in Toronto. My work at Baycrest involved sharing stories with psychiatry and palliative care patients, as well as people living with degrees of dementia. I did as much listening as telling, of course, and learned firsthand about the impact of such "storycare" on the people I met there. I hope that one day storycare will be recognized as an essential part of healthcare, especially when the people being cared for have lost—through death or illness—the ability to tell their own stories. At that point, we must become the storykeepers for our loved ones, ensuring that their memories, stories, and identities stay alive.

I started writing this chronicle about six months after Jacob's death, trying to find a way to remember, to grieve, perhaps to find a shred of meaning in this unspeakable loss. It was sparked when I was swimming—because, yes, one somehow tries to carry on, even while living in the ruins of grief—at Joseph J. Piccininni pool, the very pool where Jacob first learned to swim. I passed the waterslide and remembered how, age three, he'd come squealing down at high speed into my father's waiting arms. I began to imagine how he might tell me about those thrilling slides, and about how, as he was leaving us behind at the trauma centre so many years later, his grandfather Jack was still waiting to catch him and welcome him. With his imagined voice as my guide, I began to gather and create the texts that make up this requiem.

I've always kept a journal, and recorded many of our sons' adventures and misadventures. I kept track of all the *bons mots* they spoke, and all of the silly things they mis-spoke. Jacob, like his brother, had a great gift of language, and many of his unforgettable expressions found their way into this book. You'll also read a lot of his own writing, including a funny, moving keynote speech he gave at a Prader-Willi Syndrome fundraiser in Guelph, Ontario, two months before his death. As someone living with PWS, he faced tremendous physical and mental/ emotional obstacles growing up, especially in adolescence. He dealt with psychosis, hard-to-control weight gain, social isolation, Fournier's gangrene (successfully treated), his parents' separation, Type 2 diabetes, and the destabilizing, unrelenting hunger that is part of the syndrome. Even though he brought immense courage to these struggles, they were, at times, overwhelming. It was in his last three years that he found peace, success, responsibility, balance, friendship, stability, and a blessed job working for the Toronto Police as a crossing guard. Though you will learn about the really hard stuff he faced, these hard-won triumphs and the new life they opened are a major theme of this book. I chose to write in the present tense so you can encounter Jacob more directly, to catch a sense of him living, not of him lost. The book isn't recounted through a lens of nostalgia or reminiscence, or as a chronicle of bereavement, or as a father's attempt to repair unimaginable harm. Jacob was someone who generated stories, and his mother and brother and everyone whose lives he touched have their own vivid memories and versions of everything recounted here. This book holds only a small part of Jacob's epic story.

At Jacob's funeral his brother, Nathaniel, said something I've held on to in a heart-crushing time: love continues to exist in the world, even though his little brother has gone to be with his ancestors. Somehow, love remains.

A year after Jacob died, I did a reading of some of these stories at Itah Sadu's bookstore A Different Book List. She is another one of Jacob's many unofficial aunties. The occasion was an exhibit by our housemate and close friend Bernard Kelly featuring portraits of people wearing fedoras from Jacob's impressive collection. Jaron Freeman-Fox played fiddle, Moyo Mutamba played *mbira*, and we laughed and cried and remembered together. Afterwards, Nathaniel told me the stories should be published so more people could learn about his extraordinary little brother. My older son is my go-to wise person, so I took his advice. He reminded me that Jacob's early death is the least interesting thing about him. How he lived, the kind of man he became, is what matters, and what this book celebrates.

Two years after Jacob died, our friend Ron Evans led a ceremony in our back yard. Ron is a Metis Elder, storyteller, and tradition-keeper. He was one of Jacob's uncles, if not by blood then surely by spirit. Ron lit a fire, burned tobacco, sang honour songs, spoke of how grateful we were for having such a great soul in our lives. We burned offerings of Jacob's favourite foods (there were many, as you can guess by now) and, best of all, we told stories about him. Perhaps this book is a continuation of that ceremony, a thank-you offering made of loving words instead of carrot cake, apple pie, Jamaican roti, and Korean seafood pancakes. Ron and his partner came to live with me for a few months after Jacob died, knowing in their wisdom how much I needed a strong island in the storm of grief. When he came, he told me of a vision he'd had when he first heard about the accident—a vision of Jacob being carried gently and slowly away on the back of a great female turtle—and how that was when he knew Jacob would not survive. This vision, with Ron's permission, is near the end of the book.

Despite the tragic roots of this book, I hope that some of Jacob's astonishing wit and high spirits come through, and that you can laugh (and cry), and especially that they make you want to remember your own loved ones. It was written as a way to keep his stories alive and present, and also to encourage others to become storykeepers for your own lost beloveds.

So here is Jacob, wearing some of his many hats: as son, brother, grandson, friend, photographer, boyfriend, poet, crossing guard, dog owner, person living with a disability, advocate for all of our people who live with difference, fisher, joke-teller, jewellery-maker, St. Clair West boulevardier, collector of fedoras (and much else), games master, mensch.

I know so many things about myself that I don't actually remember but they feel real to me because I've heard the stories so often. I know that when I am born I almost die. I have an APGAR score of two. I am in the neonatal intensive care unit at the Hospital for Sick Children. No one knows what's wrong with me, and the doctors don't expect me to live. The night I am born my dad runs alongside the transfer team nurses from Toronto General to Sick Kids, and when he gets to the neonatal intensive care unit he faints. He has a vision of a procession of people carrying torches and singing in the darkness, and is so surprised that their songs were so full of joy. My mom and dad stay with me all the time. They call me their "Star Boy." They tell me that if I stick around I will come home to a nice house in a nice neighbourhood. My big brother keeps painting red flowers to tape over my crib. My dad tells me stories and reads aloud and my parents tell me that's because they didn't want my first words to be "beep beep beep." I am too weak to cry but one day when my dad and Grandpa Jack hold me in a basin for my first bath, I manage to give out a little cry. Everyone jumps for joy. My great-grandmother Florence says I am fighting so hard to stay alive because I have a purpose in life. It takes me a long time to get strong enough to crawl and strong enough to walk. But I slowly become able to do all of these things. The doctor tells my parents, just before they bring me home, "sometimes the things we don't understand clear up by themselves."

The day we come home, the Italian neighbours bring over a crostata cake. Lillian, who made the cake, carries her own death certificate because when she was born she was so weak and tiny the doctors thought she was going to die. They wrote her death certificate. Then her dad brought her back to their farm and heated up stones and put her in the middle as if she was a sick calf. She lived, but she still carries her death certificate.

My dad says that sitting by my crib in the NICU and telling me stories he felt like an air traffic controller talking to a frightened passenger who takes the controls if the pilot gets sick, teaching them to fly and land a plane they've never flown before. He says he felt like he was talking me in, trying to convince me it is a good world to be born into, one where I will find warmth and love and beauty. And I do choose to stay and the world does have all of those things.

I am two and a half and already big and my dad and brother are sitting together on the floor and they brace themselves and shout, "Boiled egg!" And I am charging into them and we all fall backwards laughing. They never tell me why they shout "Boiled egg!", and I'm not sure I ever asked. Again and again and again, laughing together as I crash into them knowing they will catch me and they always do.

I'm in the bathtub surrounded by bubbles. I'm two and a half. I scoop up them up in both hands and then they start talking to each other. My dad sometimes sits on the edge of the tub when I'm in the bath or even when I'm sitting on the toilet. He makes his hands into fists and they become two old Chinese gentlemen: Mister Hung and Mister Fang. They have long conversations while I'm sitting there. They bow to each other a lot and speak in a very polite and courtly manner. "Ah, Mister Fang, it is so very good to see you again!" "Yes, Mister Hung, it is my exceedingly great pleasure to encounter you here in Jacob's bathtub."

I am three years old and my mom and dad are singing:

Salome was a dancer
She danced the hootchy-cootch
She shook her shimmy shoulder
And she showed a bit too much
"Stop!" said King Herod
"You can't do that there 'ere!"
Salome said, "Baloney!"
And she kicked him in the rear.

It's usually after my bath, and as they sing I shake my bare shoulders, and they laugh. I don't know what "shimmy" means, but I somehow know how to do it.

When I am four years old I'm running in the front door in the evening and I trip and fall face-first onto the banister leading up to our apartment. There's blood everywhere. My dad picks me up and my mom and dad and I hurry down to St. Clair and go to the walk-in clinic. The Chinese doctor says I need stitches and my dad asks if he's good at stitches because he'll be doing it on my face, and the doctor says he's good at stitching. They hold me down and give me painkiller with a needle and they start doing the stitches. My mom is holding down my legs and my dad is holding my head. Halfway through the stitches I manage to move my mouth and say, "I hate you, doctor! You're a bum!" And then everyone starts laughing and it doesn't hurt as much, and from then on that becomes something we all say when things go wrong. My parents always say something they heard before I was born, when a French mom in a Paris garden had a baby who was crying and crying. She said: *"Ah cheri, la vie est plein d'emmerdements."* Life is full of little shittinesses.

When I am four I make up my first riddle: "What's black and red and pink and yellow and orange and grey and purple?" My parents ask, "What?" I say, "A donkey."

I'm five and there's a party at our place. It's called the Red Bean because my dad and his friend Mark Comstock, who he's known since they were teenagers, cook red beans and rice and jalapeno-cheddar-cheese-honey-cornmeal muffins and tell each other the same jokes they've been telling each other for decades. Everyone comes over to eat and sing and I stay up late. I make up a song about our first dog Mishigas. Mark Comstock and Oliver Schroer and my dad's friend Michael Pestel are all playing music as I sing:

I love her, I want to marry her
I love Mishi dear as salt
I love Mishi dear as pepper
I love her I love her she's cute
I can't wait 'til she doesn't get dead
I want to spend time with her
I hope she won't die
Boom

Now I'm six and Oliver and Soozi are playing the blues at the Red Bean, and I start to make up a song. My dad writes it down as I sing:

I want to die
And run away.

And everyone says it's the best blues line ever sung. Oliver and Soozi call me "Blues Jake." They take me to a country music night in a gay bar one night and I go onstage with them and I see so many cowboys in the audience, and I'm a little surprised.

When I'm older I'm going to sneak drinks and eat extra muffins.

"Ask me how much I love you," my dad says as he prepares my lunch.

"How much do you love me?"

"I love you so much I take the fruit tag off the pear before I give it to you."

He thinks this is funny because you're never supposed to ask people how much they love you because you shouldn't try to measure love.

I'm seven and I write a Hanukah card: "Dear family, I love you all very much so far."

Then that becomes a family saying. Everything in our family is "so far."

I'm seven and in the morning before going to school I lie on the couch holding a big rubber sword. Every morning I tell myself a story about a very strong policeman-superhero named Officer Freddie, but I pronounce it "Shreddie." And the long sword is in my hand, and I don't have to go to school for a few more minutes, and I can make the story very long and full of bad guys and danger, and I don't know yet how different I am, and nobody has told me I have something called Prader-Willi Syndrome, and for now my sword is the greatest weapon I will ever need, and I can vanquish all of my enemies. Officer Freddie is invincible. He kicks bad guys' butts.

I am seven and my teacher gives us an assignment to write a story. I write one called "The Tornado in the Jungle." The teacher gives it back and tells me I need to add more adjectives. I'm not really sure what an adjective is, but I do rewrite the story. And I give it a new title. I call it "The Tornado in the Jungle with Adjectives."

All was well in the green, planted jungle. The black, hairy gorillas were eating long, yellow bananas. The fed, scrawny monkeys were swinging in the brown, rooted trees. But most of all, the nice, black people were happy. The nice, black people lived in a small, wrecked village, named the great city of Hong Kong. The great city of Hong Kong was in the middle of the green, planted jungle. There was one greedy, little family in the village that were rich, the rest were poor. But as you know, any greedy, rich people aren't helpful. But of course poor, kind, suffering people are helpful. One day a trembling came upon the great city of Hong Kong. It was a big, twirly tornado. The big twirly tornado did a lot of damage. By the way, the great city of Hong Kong had a tough, strong army. But even the tough, strong army could not defeat the big, twirly tornado. Remember, the poor, kind, suffering people are helpful. One of the kind, suffering, poor men made a kind, suffering, poor army. Guess what … The kind, suffering, poor, tough, strong army defeated the big, twirly tornado. The kind, suffering, poor man who made a tough, strong, poor army won. The man's name was Powerful Brave John. Usually the black, nice people who win battles have courage. From that day forward there has been the great city of Hong Kong's big, twirly tornado hero Powerful Brave John. There standing while we speak is the white stone statue of Powerful Brave John. What you have just heard is the tale of the big, twirly tornado in the green, planted jungle. The End!

I am seven and my dad comes in to say goodnight and asks why my dirty socks are on the floor, and I ask him to pick them up, and he says, "Why should I pick up your dirty socks?", and I say, "Because I chose to live!"

And he laughs. But he still doesn't pick up the socks.

I am walking on St. Clair holding my father's hand. I am seven years old. I don't know it, but kids my age no longer hold their parents' hands as they walk around the neighbourhood. But I still do. There are many things about being normal that I don't know, even though I am learning that I am different. I even say to my parents, "Your son Jacob is not an ordinary person." If anyone said anything about me still holding my dad's hand at my age, I always remember what my dad says his dad used to say: "Fuck 'em!"

One day I say to my parents, "I might have been a different kid if Mom married someone else." She points out that she and my dad are common-law partners, and that she's never been married to anyone.

Learning about biology in grade one, I'm six and ask my dad: "Did you know that Mom is a mammal?" He says, "Yep, I knew that when we first started dating."

I'm seven when I realize how tough my mother is. We go to a big demonstration at Queen's Park, where the Ontario parliament building is. We are protesting cuts to education by the Mike Harris conservative government. My mom is a union leader who leads strikes by teachers. Everyone in the crowd knows her, and everyone speaks to her with a lot of respect. I already knew she is the best hugger in the world, and now I see she is also a really tough fighter for things she believes in. I'm glad she's on my side. I'd hate to bargain with her. There are police everywhere at the demonstration, but I'm not afraid because my mom's dad is a Mountie and I love police. I go behind Queen's Park with my mom and ask the riot police for their business cards because I have a collection of police business cards. Even though they have shields and batons and guns they smile at me and I bring home lots of business cards. My mom takes me to many picket lines and demonstrations that year and I grow my collection of police business cards.

One day in the locker room a kid cuts himself by accident. It reminds me of what we were chanting at the big demonstration, and I say to the people in the locker-room, "Cuts hurt kids!" Except it was just me saying it, not a hundred thousand other people shouting and raising their fists at the parliament building.

I am still seven years old, and it's the summer after grade two. We are out at Roddick Lake. We row out at dawn to the first island and are rocking up against the shore. My rod bends almost double, and my dad says, "You snagged a log." "It's a fish," I say. "Bet it's a log," he says. "Fish," I whisper, and we stay super quiet. Then the line begins to move from under the boat, and a big smallmouth bass comes leaping out of the water trying to get free. It is so beautiful. "Guess I was wrong," he says. "Glad I was wrong," he says, and nets the fish. I am so proud. And then catching so many bass and pike and releasing almost all of them after my mom or dad or camp counsellors take photos, and all the photos in the house showing fish with open mouths next to me trying to look like a fish with my mouth open. Catch and release. Catch and release. Catch and release.

I learn my grandma's pretty badass when we are at the flea market in Maniwaki on a Thursday morning. I'm seven and my grandparents have come up to visit that summer. We always go into Maniwaki on Thursdays because we get cabin fever staying in the cottage on Roddick Lake. I like to look for fishing gear and Elvis T-shirts. My grandparents look for fruit and vegetables.

I'm standing with my Grandmother Palo waiting to get blueberries and a man in front of us asks the farmer how much they cost. She answers five dollars. He argues with her, saying that's too expensive. She doesn't budge. He says, in French, "Don't be a Jew!" But he doesn't realize he's standing next to my grandmother, who speaks French and is a Jew. She turns to him and says, "*Monsieur*, you are a racist! I am Jewish. I was in the War. You must never say that again!" The man scurries away.

My grandmother stands about 5'4". She is a Holocaust survivor. I am proud of her.

My grandparents have friends in Montreal, Turkish Jews named Joseph and Herza. I'm seven when I meet them, and I call him "Jophus." My Grandpa Jack is driving with Jophus in Montreal and they stop their car as a pretty girl walks by. Jophus shakes his eighty-year-old head and says, "Mashallah ...", which means praise be to God. My dad and I, when we see someone we like on the street, say, "There goes a 'mashallah.'"

When I'm nine and a half my dad is driving me to school and we're talking about how women can surprise you. He tells me his first girlfriend had some hair on her breasts. "She showed you?" I ask. "Yes." "Why?" "Curiosity." And then I ask him, "Does Mom know?"

My dad and Grandpa Jack and I go to Heart Lake to do some fishing. I'm eight and I'm already a fisherman. My dad is on the dock and to his surprise he catches a fish. But I am even more surprised. I'm the fisherman, not him. I say, "You of all people!" My grandpa calls it Heartless Lake because we almost never catch fish there.

We go to a multicultural festival somewhere out of town when I'm eight years old, and we bring Liam Howe with us. Liam is the first person I know who has cerebral palsy. We take him swimming sometimes when I am young. He always likes to know which car we are driving. We tell him it's not the "little blue Toyota" (which we say in a tiny little voice). Then we shout that it's the "GREAT BIG HONDA!" Liam laughs with his whole body.

My dad teaches Liam a knock-knock joke, which he repeats every time we see him.

"Will you remember me tomorrow?"
"Yes."
"Will you remember me next week?"
"Yes."
"Will you remember me next year?"
"Yes."
"Knock knock."
"Who's there?"
"Did you forget me already?"

Liam LOVES to tell this joke. He uses all of his arms and legs to tell it, and it takes him a long time to get the words out, and he likes to be up close to be sure you get it.

Liam's in his wheelchair and we're looking for something good to eat. My dad and I wander over to a Chinese cook frying dumplings. The cook doesn't speak English, so he just points to the dumplings and calls out, "YUMMY YUMMY!" And we buy some and they are yummy, and after that we say "yummy yummy" whenever we find food we like.

I'm on a paddleboat from the cottage and I am fishing along the shore of Roddick Lake by myself. My favourite rod and reel slip off the paddleboat and sink into the dark water. I'm half a kilometre from our cottage, which is really the cottage of my mom's friend Frans but I have been coming since I was a baby and it feels a little like ours, too. I don't cry about losing my rod and reel even though I could. I observe the spot where they sank, noting the trees and bushes along the shore, and where I had been fishing. I go home, get my goggles and trunks, come back, dive in. I am alone. The water is very dark, and I'm past the dropoff, and it's deep here. I dive and I dive and I dive and I dive, and then I find the rod and reel on the mucky, murky bottom. I am alone in the dark water, and I find my lost rod and reel. This is a very, very hard thing to do.

When I am little and hug my Grandpa Jack my nose reaches his *pupik*. His old sweater smells like potage. He makes the best potage and I smell the potage on his old sweater. I have a very good sense of smell. He also makes blueberry pancakes just for me. I am so scared to go visit him when he is dying in the hospital at Baycrest. It is strange to see such a strong man flat on his back. He used to take me on his motorcycle and now he can't move. I go to visit him on my ninth birthday and he can still smile, even with a tube in his nose, and he can still whisper, "Happy Birthday, Jakeronomous" and he hands me an envelope with $100 in it. I find out later my grandma prepared it for him so he'd be able to give me a gift to celebrate my birthday. And they tell me that it is the last thing he says before he slips into a coma and dies five days later. Almost a year later on Father's Day I tell my Grandmother Palo, "I'm lucky because I can celebrate Father's Day—and my dad can celebrate Heaven Day." I'm not sure she understands. But my dad does. He really loved his dad. Me too.

My other grandpa, Jim, loves fedoras as much as me. We both collect hats. He is a pistol shot champion, and there's a photo of him and his gun and my mom when she was little. Grandpa Jim is pretty fussy about being clean and tidy. He's also not very touchy-feely. I ask him, "Would you mind if the material of your suit got wrinkled if I hugged you?" He says, "Yes." I tell him, "Too bad!" and hug him and he laughs and hugs me back. I'm eleven. When he is dying he tells us he wished he had shown us more love, but I always knew he loved me even if he didn't give out hugs very often, or kisses either. He doesn't like to get his hands dirty and he has sayings that make me laugh. Once he is talking about some asshole he knew when he was a Mountie, and he says, "I wouldn't piss down his throat if his guts were on fire." I guess he really didn't like the guy very much.

My dad's mother is Romanian, and tells jokes about how Romanians are such tricky people.

We're at the Ashkenaz Jewish music festival and I ask my dad, "Dad, are there any Romanian holidays we could celebrate?" He says, "Probably. Why?" "So I could skip school and steal two eggs." I'm eleven. The Romanian cake recipe starts like that: steal two eggs. That's what my Grandma Palo says.

One day at Humewood School I play a joke. I have a scar running down the middle of my head from when I was a baby and they had to open up my skull to let my brain grow. One day I tell a grade two kid the scar was from a bear biting my head in a fight. He believes me. It's a better story than just saying a doctor cut it open. You can see it when I shave my head. I usually bring a gigantic carrot—at home we call it a "country" carrot—and a half a head of lettuce to lunch in grade six at Humewood School. The other kids make fun of me and call me a rabbit, so I quit bringing all that lettuce to school. It's too hard to explain that I'm always hungry.

When I'm in grade five at McMurrich Public School I'm always getting into trouble. My teacher may have been a good correctional services officer but she is a lousy teacher. One day I'm rude, and she makes me write a letter apologizing, and then the vice-principal makes me write another letter. Then I tell the vice-principal, "That's as sorry as I can get."

I am eleven years old and a bit of a mischief-maker. My French teacher gives me a punishment—she calls it a "consequence"—for "excessive talking while Seth should be working, ignoring teacher while she is speaking, carrying a conversation while teacher is administering instructions." I write this paragraph 20 times.

Respecter: v.a. Honorer, reverer, porter respect. Respecter la vieillesse, respecter la qualité. Faire attention a quelqu'un, quelque chose.

I think teachers who give out punishments should be punished.

My first dog Mishigas is eight. I write her autobiography for my grade six class at Humewood.

P.S. and Me (as told to Jacob Yashinsky-Zavitz)

Hi— I'm Mishigas. I'm a Jewish city dog. My human family called me Mishigas because I'm very crazy. Mishigas means "crazy" in Yiddish. I was born in a pen on a farm. I don't remember my parents very well, but I know I had a sister and three brothers. I was cuddling with my family in the pen one day, when all of a sudden a family of four walked in. Odd giant creatures they were, for I think they were humans. A little boy walked up to the fence, and I knew that it was destined for him to be my P.S. I felt warmth of love and happiness and walked over to my future P.S. family. The boy pulled me out and it felt so nice to be held. While I was in his arms I noticed something quite odd. There was a strange smell to him, for he did not smell like family. Because of his unusual smell I call him U.S.P., which means "unusually smelly puppy." I've got many other nicknames for him, like Snackbringer or P.S. (puppy servant).

My P.S. took me outside, and it was so bright it blinded my eyes. The ground underneath me was cold, unlike the floor of the pen I slept in. It was white, and I was sliding on it. I'm so glad P.S. was there to help me. I was carried in this thing that was roaring with a loud sound, taking me somewhere I was not familiar with.

I arrived in a very unusual and slightly scary place, far bigger than the fields surrounding my farm. It had great tall, gigantic things and structures that were still. There were so many of them, as many as my eyes could see. Whatever these things were, they scared me. So what I said to myself to get over my fright was "Imagine how fun it will be to pee on them!"

When I got closer in to the city, I noticed there were dozens of the same things I was carried in, those loud roaring things. The deeper into the place, the louder it got, till it was booming in my head creating migraines of painful suffering. The air was quite different than the farm's, it was not clean or fresh. It was not nice to breathe, it was dirty air that I couldn't breathe. This created a problem, because I didn't think I could live here.

I'm now eight years old, and I've unbelievably found a way to live here. Living in the city actually isn't so bad, for I achieved something I didn't think I could do, I adapted to city life. The tall giant structures don't scare me anymore because they mark my territory. And I've gotten used to the environment. And the transporting things no longer give me a reason to *noodge* (that's Yiddish for 'whine') about my migraines. Everything's great, and I'm happy and fortunate to live in the city.

While living in the city I've had a lot of fun. P.S. takes me on walks to the park every day, when P.S. isn't in school. I'm set free in the park and I can run anywhere I want. Parks are beautiful, full of trees and birds and people. I enjoy smelling their crotches, it's one of the things I do best. Sometimes P.S. takes me to way bigger parks. There are trees, forests, swamps, and dogs. When I go to this place I like to jump in the swampy water and drink from there. It's dirty water, but water's water, and drinking from swamps is part of my dog nature. I love this place because it reminds me of the farm I lived in in my early childhood.

Spending time with P.S. is what I love doing best. Sometimes I roll over and he rubs my stomach and blows on it. When he does it I get all excited and bark, but it's really quite relaxing. Sometimes early in the morning I run downstairs and jump on P.S.'s bed. I lick his face so damn well he doesn't need to take a shower. I lick my P.S.'s face, till the point he cries for help or yells "Mercy!" Most of the time I spend with P.S. is to train him to do what I say by command. If I want him to pick up my toy I say "RRRR!" or whine the most awful sound you have ever heard a dog make!

I'm way smarter than P.S., for I'm the boss. Sometimes I stand for hours with the ball in front of him, standing up, watching his every move, waiting for him to throw it. I like doing that a lot because it's very irritating and it pisses him off. Well, those are things I like doing best with P.S., and those are my happy memories that I'll always cherish within me.

My life's not always so gleeful. I've experienced some painful and frightening memories too. Once as a pup I was taken to a very scary place. I was surrounded with humans in blue uniforms who wore white masks. That was not fun at all when they came at me with these sharp long needles. Ughhh. And one time I was on a walk during winter, I was running and something stuck up in the bottom of my paw. It was bleeding consistently, leaving red gruesome tracks. Whatever it was it stung my cut! I had to get it bandaged up and I wore a huge funnel over my head. A while back ago I was running in Hillcrest Park around the tennis courts, when all of a sudden this huge mixed husky came out from behind a tree and attacked me. It took a big chunk out of my side, and it was hard to get out of my crate in the morning. Even the loving and sweet persuasive voice of P.S. couldn't get me out. When my family found out about my injury, I was rushed to the hospital. I had to get stitches and they shaved one of my sides. I felt like a naked poodle. Those were some bad days.

When I was quite young I had a growing pain in my hind legs. It kept me back from doing old tricks and jumping over benches but most of all it kept me back from my everyday routines, and I became less energetic and active. Well, that's the down side of my life, and when I look back I realize that without P.S., and my loving human family and my one dog friend, Cosmo, I would never have gotten through those hard times.

My dad and I are driving down Bathurst near Front Street, and there's a fancy sports car dealership on the east side, and I see a Lamborghini in the window. I love expensive cars. I yell, "LamborGHINI!!!" and my dad jumps as he's driving. I'm twelve. Then, even after the shop is gone, whenever we drive down Bathurst we laugh and shout, "LamborGHINI!" And sometimes we just shout it to make each other jump.

I always beat my dad at games. One day we play Scrabble and I get a bunch of triple words and wind up with 568. He has 257. He saves the piece of paper and shows everyone my score. I also beat him at Boggle, and at Monopoly, and at backgammon, and at Settlers of Catan. We play Monopoly, even though it's always hard for just two people to play Monopoly because you can go back and forth so many times without anyone winning. But I'm a really good Monopoly player and my dad is really bad. So I wind up with all the good properties and I build hotels, and he keeps landing on them. When I have $8,000 and he has $94 I say, "Shall we take a moment to count our money?" We laugh so hard we cry.

Sometimes he takes revenge on me by talking slang. It makes me cringe. "Yo', dude," he says, and I say: "Stop talking modern!" He does it to annoy me. "Yo', homie, I'm down with that." Slang just doesn't sound right when old people say it. It's just wrong in so many ways.

It is the seder just after my bar mitzvah, and my grandmother's cousin Bibi is visiting from Tel Aviv. I am wearing my dark blue bar mitzvah suit, and a shirt and tie. But I'm not wearing socks or shoes. My grandmother Palo is not happy that I'm barefoot at the seder but Bibi just laughs and says, "Don't worry, Palombica. When the Jews had to leave Egypt in a hurry, who had time to put their shoes on?" And Bibi always says something that we say now, with an Israeli accent: "What can you do?" And then we always do a Jewish shrug. At that seder I sneak outside near the end, and then come through the front door like Elijah saying, "I hear there's an extra cup of wine!"

I'm twenty-five before I finally learn to like my grandma Palo. We're in her living room after supper, and my dad says he's going to go do the dishes. She says, "Leave it, man!" We all laugh. I never thought she could sound hip. She is an eighty-eight-year-old Holocaust survivor. From then on, I'm nice to her and she's nice to me and I even say to my dad one day, "I never thought I'd actually look forward to visiting Grandma Palo."

I buy my Hobie Pro Angler kayak with my bar mitzvah money. I pedal it for hours across any lake we go to. I can stow six rods in the rod holders, and keep a stringer attached to the side, and keep my tackle box within easy reach, and keep water and lunch and snacks handy. My favourite boat is my Hobie because it's completely quiet, which is what you need for fishing.

Before my Hobie Pro Angler we use a v-stern canoe with a Torqueedo electric motor on it. Before that we have a regular canoe and put a bracket on the back for our motor.

Before that we have a Walker Bay dinghy, which is very comfortable and very stable and we use a two-stroke Honda motor for it. My dad isn't very good at looking after motors, and he burns out one of our boat motors by not checking the oil.

Before that we have a boat called Visitation. My dad gets it from a minister who named it that so if he went fishing his wife could tell his parishioners, if they call asking him to come over, that he is out on "visitation."

Before we start to buy our own boats we use the old rowboat that Frans keeps in the yard at the cottage. It leaks, and after a while my dad always has to row back as fast as he can so we don't sink.

One day my Grandpa Jack, my dad, and I go out into the middle of the lake. My grandpa catches a big bass. He is the kind of guy who likes fishing but doesn't really like catching fish. He looks so surprised as he hauls up his line and sees a big fish dangling on his hook. My dad takes the fish off the hook. We bring it back to shore and kill it. My dad leaves it by the back door while he cleans up and gets ready to make supper. When he comes out after supper the fish is gone. Turns out our dog Mishigas has picked it up and moved it down the stone steps. Even though it has teeth marks on it, we still fillet it and eat it the next day.

I write a letter from Camp Couchiching. It's the summer before I get into really big trouble there.

Dear Mommy and Daddy,

So far I'm having a great time. The girls are sweet and beautiful, and one from what I hear likes me. I've made a lot of friends. There is one named Mat, he's such a pothead, smokes by the ounce with his rastafari friend, he's cool most of the time but makes fat jokes and says I could fish with my nipples. It's annoying sometimes. Stephen's cool still, but it's different. I feel that he changes at camp. There is a Filipino kid named Paul, he smuggled Chinese from a meal into a bag and brought it to the cabin. It was hilarious. There's Andrew, who is such a cool kid, and 1 of 3 black people this year. It's weird how it's mostly white. I made friends with him right away. And then there's the rest of the kids in the cabin that I don't really talk to. On Wednesday I caught a 4 ½ lb. largemouth bass. It was awesome. I'll tell you the story and all about it when I see you. There is only two things I ask of you for my return. Bring my beloved Mishigas and plz get me a pair of earphones for my cd player. I need them for our Quebec trip. I only threw away the old earphones because they didn't work anymore. Well, I have to go do my activities for the day. I hope you enjoy this letter, cuz I didn't get one from u. And Zac says hi, he's the only real Jew in the cabin besides me.

Love, Jacob

Whenever he writes to me at camp or from his trips my dad always signs his letters: Love, Paaaa. It's from a joke our friend Jamie Oliviero told us once.

A man is driving along in the back country and passes a hill. There's a man on the hill having sex with a sheep. The man is really upset when he sees this, and drives down into the valley to where there's a broken-down old farmhouse. There's a little kid playing in the front yard.

"I need to use your phone!" the man says.

"Oh heck, Mister, we don't have a phone out here. We're too poor. What's the problem?"

"I've just seen something terrible. There's a man down the road having sex with a sheep!"

The little boy said, "Don't worry about that. It's just Paaaaaa."

I am thirteen and writing a lot of poetry, which I perform every week at the Marie Shchuka Library open mic. I write a long poem called "Life", but I never read it to anyone but my parents because it is so long.

Life

Sometimes I wonder what's the point of life,
and here I lie at night,
looking up at the stars so bright
giving off their golden light,
there they are floating in the air
and they make me think and stare—
why was I brought into the world
looking as a ball and curled
like something someone could hurl,
for there I was in my mom's uterus,
giving her joy and bliss,
then suddenly it dropped
and out of her I hopped,
sick as a baby
none to save me
but I chose to stay alive
and there I was in the hospital for weeks,
probably even five—
I came home at last,
no flags at half-mast,
and settled in just finely,
if you don't mind me saying I think quite frankly
my parents were completely friendly—
so then with them I grew up, with a brother
and a crazy pup
and here I am now still thinking of life
looking at the stars at night
I zoomed past childhood like the blink of an eye
without even flying a kite—
but did I tell you the time I took a fall...

down the stairs in pairs,
my lip was stitched
and it hurt like a bitch
and I called the doctor a bum
stitching my lips that weren't even numb—
and then went down my thumb
for I was not happy
and was in need of a taffy—
that's when PW kicked in,
ashamed and born with a sin
stealing cookies out of the cookie tin
growing so fat not even thin
I'll live unhappily forever and ever
for if born without PW I'd feel and live better
so here I am with an eating disorder
One in a thousand kids
and I was the one god picked me for this
and I don't rejoice with bliss
I hate this curse
it gets worse and worse
maybe as far as a hearse
god forbid that will happen
for I am a mild case
kids like me would run and run for a normal life to chase—
don't think everything is horrible just 'cause of what I write
'cause my poetry is deep and can give you a fright
it makes you visualize the graphics
no matter way I write this
but most of it is true
I've gone through bad times just like you
for all the bad times I write them in my rhymes
to express my feeling within,
sometimes to let go of bad sins
to let it all out in a flow to my paper
feeling what I feel and let go
so through my poetry my feelings will show
and to my knowledge it will grow.

my life doesn't suck
it's really quite great
'cause I share one of life's most treasurous pleasures
to have family and friends to hang with for leisure
and I love them all at great measures
I'll love them forever and ever and as I once said "so far"—
like my grandpa living in the skies shining in heaven like the
stars.
for I'll cherish my memories that I have of him
as long as I live from that day,
when I turned nine and he passed away
watching his remains decay
for he's part of earth now
in a happier place,
and still he looks upon me
I feel his presence and race and race
hoping he'll still be there
but then he leaves back to the heavens without even leaving a
trace
his death saddened me,
and brought tears to me
and is still gone to this day
and every day I think of him more and more
and every time I remember him my heart grows sore and sore
gramps was special to me
and god took him from me
and I loved him with all my heart
and writing about him in my poems you see, is my talent what
you people call art.
he always was there for me during the roughest times
and now I wish he were right by my side,
cheering my feelings inside.
not every grandpa feeds you mickey dees and serves you
blueberry pancakes
there was a connection between me and gramps
that no one could ever make
I hope he is happy wherever he is

and watch me grow up in bizz
but enough of Gramps, I can't praise him all day, or cry
over his early death,
for I have other things to worry about in this day and age
for it is not rage for I feel love, for a woman as sweet as
a dove. I don't know what I feel, is the feeling of love
but I like this girl very much, in many ways
like such
she's pretty and funny and makes me laugh
and is good at all subjects including math
her humour is great,
and in her I have faith
for I like her a lot
and when I think of her I put into thought
I sought love would be true
but as I thought it's totally not
at age 13 I don't feel love
but the likeness for girls
for instance you
I have I have I have
but deep down inside me it might be love 'cause I
like you more and more
and when not in your company my heart grows sore
down to the bitter aching core,
I'm not sure it's love that I feel for you,
I think it's because you are a great friend
since you e-mail me and press send
so our friendship across T.dot won't end
I thank you for the friendship you gave me
for I'll take it wherever I go
and I give you mine in return for yours
thank you for your generosity,
still being friends, creating no democracy,
by the way, politics suck, because who's running
these days, these politicians can't run our city
for they're leading it to solemn destruction,
most took away our city's pride

and put a lot of peeps on streets as beggars
and they live quite opposite of famous Mick Jagger
for all day they beg for money
and their lifestyles ain't even funny—
what do the politicians and mayor do about this
I'll tell you and it's true: jack shit—
for it's them who did this to our city
and they make us look bad with shame and pity
and why are they famous? they can't lead our nation
I hope the politicians suffer constipation
so how 'bout we put them on the streets to suffer salvation
to experience life they did to the poor
and to see how they affect
the T.dot Nation to prove my political accusation
well, these are the things society suffers and as I say "bad times"
and here I am spitting my message to you
And hopefully I will reach you through rhymes
I'm trying to tell you people bad things are happening around us
so I'm telling you now I think we must
step up and help those peoples
for they're walking the streets drunk on their feet
no home to go to at night,
so help some out, give out a hand
show no fright and respect them
for they are kind and part of our population
and sadly a sad part of distribution
so when christmas comes make a resolution
and help the people in need
give a quarter or food to feed on
and then you'll fulfill your deed
do it for a year, and you'll feel better inside,
so your pride won't collapse and collide
for we are a society "T. dot" nation that should always give a
hand and share,
so help the poor, that compared to ours, their life is never fair.
well these are the problems our city has these days
and I'm 13 and I've observed

so don't be greedy and selfish
'cause not everything in society is self-serve
and stop this racism, sexism, and violence
and don't live the laws in defiance
'cause there's too much in the world this day and age
and violence leads to war
look at Israel and Palestine
it used to be peaceful and fine
now they're fighting for land
they're all good people
but their evil streak deceives them
so please stop it, I'm just asking
or is that too much of a tasking?
well these are the good and the bad things in life
so don't fight back in anger and strife
make society peaceful again
and don't forget that women are as equal as men
as much as I love writing poetry
I must end it in these last words
for these are my memoirs and still a future to come
and I hope my message to some
will be of an actual meaning
and not a pointless poem
I don't know what I want to be when I'm older
but one thing for sure
Imma still keep writing and present it bolder
I don't know what I want to be when I'm older
an accountant, jeweller, or fisher,
but for my fantasy to come true
I must be a wisher
to wish on the stars shining bright
when I think what's the point of life
in this particular dark star-light night.

I'm fourteen and home from camp for my birthday on August 20, 2005. But when I go to my room I see someone has opened my safe and taken away two air pistols I'd bought with my own money. My parents didn't know about them. I am so angry with my father when he tells me he took them away and I shouldn't have had them in the first place. But then after telling him I hated him so much, later that night we are walking to get a birthday ice cream and he tells me how much he loves me, and how much my mom loves me, and how much my brother loves me, and I start to cry and I tell my dad all of the bad things I've been keeping secret. I cry and cry and talk and talk, and it feels good. I tell him what it feels like to live in the shadows and to sometimes not want to be alive at all because of feeling so ashamed. And when we look at the full moon I say, because I know how native people give names to each moon, "That's the truthful moon." And it feels so good to be open for a change.

We once saw a movie where someone says, "You're only as sick as your secrets." I get that. But it's hard not to keep secrets if you have Prader-Willi Syndrome. I loved those guns. My Grandpa Jim was an Olympic pistol shot champion, so maybe it runs in the family.

But my troubles are not over. It is so hard. I have a weird dark bump on my finger. It doesn't really hurt, but that's because I have a high pain threshold, like most people with Prader-Willi Syndrome. When they finally take me to our doctor after camp, the doctor cuts in and finds the barbed end of a fish-hook that had been stuck in my finger and turned black. I am so happy when it is taken out. All that summer at camp I keep looking at this ominous dark-green-mostly-black spot and feel so weird because I don't know what is causing it.

And that summer everything goes wrong. I steal things. I am bullied. I take stuff from my counsellors and then I run away to the resort next door and take stuff from people's rooms. My adolescent Prader-Willi Syndrome hunger drives me crazy. And

I beg my parents to pick me up because I know I'm going to do really bad shit, but they don't. I come back for my birthday then go back to camp hell. Then when I finally get home, I send my parents this e-mail on August 28, 2006. My dad tells a story called The Devil's Noodles, and I use it in my letter. It's a folktale about the time the Devil and his sons show up at a restaurant in Little Italy, and Renato the chef tricks them all using a frying pan, a spinning chair, and the freezer where he keeps the wine he sells without a liquor licence. I know the story by heart and it's what comes to my mind as I write about my summer of pain and devilry, and ask for help.

i've enjoyed camp for many years as we all know but this session was not the greatest. the last week of camp i felt i was falling apart. arguments about food. at times i felt starved, not getting my bronze med which i worked hard to get. i felt like I failed myself. i turned against pretty much all the staff because i didn't feel like you really know me. i don't really know myself either. i've been happy most of my life and i'm surprised that i did those stupid things. i know this is kind of silly but I'm thinking that the green spot on my finger is a spot of evil. and I sometimes think it's going to spread and take over my good soul. i am kind of a vagabond and renato would probably put me in a frying pan, a spinning chair, and a freezer. although i wud probably drink all the "grapejuice" before i wud be frozen. and I gamble like renato but in a different way. i gambled in life not game and risked all your trust which i might have lost. i'm talking to you in this email because i know it wud be hard for me to talk to you in person. that day at bronze med i called you indeed. i told you to come get me but nobody listened. i knew i was going to do stupid things and i was trying to prevent it before my bad conscience was overpowering. when I needed you the most there you ignored me and didn't take me home. i'm not blaming you on this in any way because it was all my fault and i'm the one to blame. and i need you guys now more than i needed you both at camp.

i hope you didn't tell the rest of the family about my adventures at camp. i need to know that you didn't tell natty about the stolen camera, or my grandparents. the last thing i want to do is disappoint them especially after i disappointed myself and you guys.

things you want to know:

the knives weren't found at Town Hall. i know you know where I got them. i'm embarrassed to say. the necklace was found at the same place.

i am really sorry i apologize completely on behalf of what i fucked up on. and i'm asking for help.

—Jacob

I read *Kayak Angler* magazine, *Bass* magazine, Dan Savage's sex advice column in *NOW*, Nikon manuals, Armistead Maupin's books about San Francisco. After reading *Tales of the City* I tell my parents, "This story is so weaved!" I also read Mark Haddon's book about a boy with autism, and some Dick Francis novels, and a short story called "What We Talk About When We Talk About Love." I write an essay about that story for my English class, and get an A+. The cardiologist in that story knows all about hearts and nothing about love. I read lots of joke books, especially ones with Jewish jokes.

When I'm ten years old my dad and I are at a café so he can write his book and I can write a story. "It's all in the pencil!" I say, ten years old. Then I ask him, "Are you still writing about your life?"

When I'm young I take things literally. The grade one teacher has been reading "Puss in Boots" aloud. I come home and retell it to my parents. When I get to the line "The King smacked his lips," I take my hand and smack my lips. They explain that it's just an expression, and that it doesn't actually mean smacking your lips. I'm relieved.

When I'm fourteen I write a poem in praise of rice cakes:

Rice Cake

A puffy treat of desire
Cooked over an open fire
Toasting from heat
Forming a treat
With a taste of blissful sweetness
Roasting to the colour of gold
Warming your insides from the exterior cold
A cake of delicious rice tasteful like paradise
A moment of grace
With our community of varied race
This dessert grain laced with a sugary paste
Creates memory to remember and hold forever
That night surrounded by warmth and fire
Enjoying that puffy cake desire.

Once when I notice my hair is picking up blond highlights during my fourteenth summer, I tell my parents, "I'm turning into a potato!" The reason I say that is from a joke my friend Stephen told. A blonde, a brunette, and a redhead broke into a grocery store. The alarm went off and they ran into the alley and hid in some old produce sacks. The police arrived with their flashlights and saw the sacks. They kicked the one with the brunette, and she said, "Meow," so the cops said, "Must be a cat in that sack." They kicked the one with the redhead and she said, "Woof woof!" "Must be a dog." They kicked the one with the blonde in it and she said, "Po-ta-to."

I giggle as I read joke books in the bathroom when I'm on the toilet. My dad hears me in the kitchen and knows I'll come out with a new joke. This is my favourite:

Saul is at his store one day and he hears a voice from on high: "SAUL! SELL YOUR BUSINESS!" He ignores the voice, but it keeps speaking to him. So he sells his business for three million dollars.

The voice speaks again: "SAUL! TAKE YOUR MONEY AND GO TO LAS VEGAS!" So he goes.

And the voice says: "SAUL! GO TO THE CASINO AND GO TO THE BLACKJACK TABLE!" He goes to the blackjack table and the voice says: "SAUL! PUT IT ALL ON ONE HAND!" He is so nervous, but he bets all three million dollars on one hand. He is dealt an 18. The dealer has a 6 showing.

"SAUL! TAKE A CARD!" "But I'm already at 18," he whispers.

"TAKE A CARD!" says the voice. So he tells the dealer to hit him, and he draws an ace.

And the voice says: "SAUL! TAKE ANOTHER CARD!" He can't believe it, but he asks for another card. He draws another ace. Now he's at 20.

"SAUL! TAKE ANOTHER CARD!" "C'mon," he tells the voice, "I'm already at 20!"

"SAUL …"

So he says to the dealer, "Hit me." A third ace. He's at 21. He wins.

And the voice says, "UN-BE-FUCKING-LIEVABLE!"

My dad tells me I do a good God voice.

My second favourite joke that I like to tell my dad but don't think I can tell my mom:

A blind man goes into a restaurant and tells the waiter, "I won't be able to read the menu but I have an excellent sense of smell. Just bring me a dirty fork from the kitchen and I'll know what you're cooking today."

The waiter brings a used fork, the customer smells it and says, "I'll have the spaghetti and meatballs, please."

Same thing happens the next day. "I'd like to have the veal with a caesar salad."

After a few more days, the waiter mentions it to the owner. The owner is a little surprised and very curious. He decides to play a trick on the blind customer. He gives a fork to his wife and asks her to rub it between her thighs.

The next day the waiter brings the fork to the man. He smells it and says, "I didn't know Angela works here."

I am fourteen, almost fifteen, and our friends Pearl and Hans and their two daughters Emma and Cato are visiting from Holland. My grandmother was on her way over when the Dutchies were visiting, and I told Emma, "She's going to tell me everything that's wrong and then praise my jewellery." Hans always makes me laugh. Once we were all walking on a trail in Algonquin Park, and we were teasing him about what his name would be if he were a bird: "The Dutch beer-bellied hooter." He is one of the only people in the world who makes my dad laugh until he snorts and cries and slides off his chair.

Emma and Cato are like my sisters, and we are talking when one of the grown-ups comes too close. I say, "This is an embarrassment-free zone!" and the grown-ups laugh and leave.

One day Emma says something that we keep as a saying in our family: "We've learned something new today, and that's a beautiful thing."

There is a trout pond near Bouchette, Quebec, and every summer we drive there to catch a few trout for dinner. Here's the best thing about it. You take your trout to the lady in the wooden shed. She kills it by bending its head back and cracking the spine. Then she guts it and pulls the heart out and cuts it loose. She puts the heart on the wooden board and we all stand around to watch it keep beating, even though it isn't attached to the fish any more. It seems like a miracle to see the heart of a trout beating like that. Or a great mystery. How is it possible?

I am trying to understand all of the mysteries around me and in me. But it's hard. I become a philosopher with more questions than answers. Once, driving back from fishing with my dad, I spend many kilometres tapping my lower lip while I am humming. My dad turns his head and gives me a puzzled look and I say, "If I had an explanation I would give it to you."

One day my dad and my mom and I are strolling through New York. We are ambling along. Sometimes it drives them crazy how slowly I walk, but this time we are all taking our time enjoying the sights and sounds. I tell my parents, "The slower I walk, the more I see." My dad answers, "Does that mean if you stop walking, you'll see the most?"

We're in a bar in the Old City in Montreal. I'm fourteen and my dad and I have come to a storytelling festival. He's busy talking to the other storytellers and I figure it's my big chance to get a beer. He doesn't notice me order a pint. The bartender doesn't bat an eye, just serves me. I bring it back to the table. It takes a little while for my dad to notice what I've done, and I just sit there sipping my beer while all the adults keep talking. Then he sees me, and he laughs, and I get to drink the beer, and Montreal is my favourite city after that. I think the beer is called Le Trou du Diable. I feel very grown-up.

When I was five, someone at kindergarten asked me, "Why are you so fat?" I said, "Because of all the beer I drink." And here I am nursing a pint in Montreal at age fourteen.

I'm on my way to high school when I realize I've forgotten the jewellery a teacher at West Toronto wants to look at. It's the last day before March Break, and my parents are driving me. We're most of the way to school, and I'm so upset, crying even. I say, "If only I'd made this mistake yesterday!" But we fix it. They drop me off at school and go back home and bring the jewellery down later that morning, and the teacher likes it, and buys a piece. It's a strange concept even for me, who says it.

I am always wondering about stuff. I have lots of questions. "Why" is my favourite word.

"What's a 'fimble'?" I ask, when I'm five years old. My mom says, "Use it in a sentence." So I say, again, "What's a 'fimble'?" A question is a sentence. We finally figure out I mean 'thimble.' I wonder about words a lot.

I'm seven years old and sitting in the bathtub and doing more wondering. My dad is sitting nearby. "There are two legends about the tooth fairy," I tell him. "One is that it's your parents, the other one is that it's the tooth fairy." And once when we went to McDonald's I ask, "'Scuse me … why doesn't people at McDonald's never really smile?

When I'm nine my dad is in the living room doing a weird dance I've never heard of called a rhumba. I say, "Are you just trying to dance or are you dancing?"

When I am fourteen, my dad and I are watching *The Godfather*, and I have so many questions about the Corleone family, and why they murder each other. He does his Jewish voice and says, "God, why did you give me such an inquisitive son?" And I say, "What's 'inquisitive'?"

I'm fourteen and in New York, and we are visiting the Nuyorican Poets Café, in Alphabet City. We come early in the afternoon just so we'd know where it is, and a drunk guy is sleeping across the threshold. We step over him and find the owner, who is also pretty high. He says we'll be able to get in for sure that night because, "everyone gets in."

When we come back that night there's a long line, and we get in. A girl behind us says there's a nice spoken word event in New Jersey she goes to. The boy in front of us says, "I don't do New Jersey." The emcee keeps saying, "Bring up the en-ergy!" and it gets a bit irritating because the crowd is already super-excited.

We hear a poet named Lemon, who had just come out of Rikers Island jail.

Later that evening I volunteer to do a poem. It's about 1 am. I read "Me and My Poetry," which I wrote for an open mic in Toronto. People clap, and the girl who goes to New Jersey is still there and she's smiling, and my dad does his embarrassing fingers-in-his-mouth whistle, and then we walk all the way back to where we're staying, and I am proud that I did a poem in New York City.

Me and My Poetry

Basically, my life moves by melody lyrically.
The basics, the base of me
Is what brings me out the most
My roots stand me up straight,
But my poetry is my soul mate
Like ballistics
In the air
Ideas flare
And rhymes come to mind
What I find
Is that poetry defines what I feel

Releases my mind to a relaxed deal
Of purity
Emotions, reflections, reactions, and imperfections
I feel the same things you do
I get moods
Of
Romance, a cloudy trance,
Rainy thoughts
But whatever inflects my inner self
I feel I ought
To jot
Every feeling, itch, or my self being doubt I got.
My technique and critique
is what makes me unique.
Sure I may be mystic
But that's my physics
Like hieroglyphics, it says "write"
I've done it for ages
Moving to different stages
To some, how to rhyme is a mystery
But the gift came to me in early history
Cause my destiny knew I had to be a poet
I just know it
So the talent I picked up before
Still being stored
Poetry is still the artform, expression, depression, reflection
Or just the only way to bring out aggression.
I know, poetry is that path I chose
Where I have to go
And what shows
How my feelings grow
But whatever happens
Who knows
My poetry is what makes me me
My human being to be
Poetry and me.

My friend Daniel Kennedy takes a photo of me in our photography class. I'm wearing a black coat, my head is shaved, and a cigarette is stuck in the corner of my mouth. I am making a fist like a real tough guy, and the way he shoots the photo my fist is so close to the camera it looks huge. All in all, I look pretty badass.

I did punch a wall once, on a locked ward, but never punched a person.

My brother says it's his favourite photo of me.

One summer I go to sit on the seat of my Hobie Pro Angler kayak and it breaks. My dad says it's probably because he put it in wrong. This is a fancy, fancy seat and it cost me $600 of my own money. We take it back to Fogh Marine and they replace it on warranty, although they say they've never had one break before. I notice my dad keeps pretty quiet about how it might have happened. Then the same thing happens again, and the metal tube on one side snaps when I sit on it. This time my dad asks a friend of his in Peterborough if he knows a welder, and his friend tells him to go to Wayne. He takes the seat to Wayne the welder, an old guy with a barnful of tools. I wasn't there but my dad tells me what happened. Wayne didn't think he could fix it. "Wouldn't know where to put the weld," he said. But after a few days he called my dad up and said, "I fixed it. Last night I had a dream, and I saw where to put the weld. It's been like that for fifty years. The dreams help me fix stuff." The seat doesn't break again, no matter how many times I sit on it. And we talk about this eighty-year-old welder near Peterborough who listens to his dreams. We just have to say "Wayne the Welder" and we know we're talking about dreams that come true.

These are my rods:

G. Loomis.
Shimano.
Kistler.
Daiwa.
Quantum.
Lamiglas.
Streamside.
Fenwick.
Megabass.
St. Croix.
Pflueger.
Zebco from when I was little and didn't know much about gear.

I call them my weapons of bass destruction. I sometimes rig them up with different reels and practise casting in my bedroom, or even just holding them to feel how balanced they are.

These are my reels:

Daiwa Pixy.
Shimano Currado.
Shimano Calcutta Conquest.
Shimano Chronarch.
Shimano Scorpion.
Shimano Metanium.
Shimano Stradic.
Daiwa Zillion.
Pflueger President.
Abu Garcia Ambassadeur.
Quantum Energy.
Quantum Pt.
Quantum Tour Edition.
Alpha 103L.
Ryobi Applause.

I'm fifteen the summer my dog Mishigas dies. I'm out fishing on Shadow Lake when my dad drives up to camp. He and I go out on a paddleboat and do some fishing together before driving home. Shadow Lake has bass and pike, and I'm one of the only campers who likes to fish there. He waits until we're back on the shore, and sits down next to me outside the Shadow Lake mess hall, and puts his arm around me, and tells me my dog died. Mishi had to be put down—she was very sick. He tells me she died in his arms, looking up at him. Mishi was my first dog. We bought her from a farmer. When she was a puppy she bit me, but I forgave her. I love her so much, and even my mom ended up loving her.

For the last couple of years we mainly had her on weekends because my grandmother needed her to help her not go crazy with grief for my Grandpa Jack. So she stayed with her during the week. When my dad tells me the news, I cry more for Mishi than I did for my grandpa, who I also loved a lot but I was only eight when he died.

Mishi is a border collie, and the fastest dog in the park. She can even go up and down the slide. A day after getting back from Shadow Lake, my parents drive me to Pittsburgh, to get treatment at the Prader-Willi Syndrome hospital. I lose weight there, but hate it, and miss my family and miss my dog. Everybody on the ward looks for extra food all the time. Once I get so mad I smash my hand against the wall, and the punishment is they tell my mom she can't take me out of the hospital even though she drives seven hours to visit me. My brother comes once, just to see me, and I am so happy. I live there for seven and a half weeks, and lose a bunch of weight, and when I come home there are locks on the fridge and freezer and pantry. That's how you know it is a Prader-Willi Syndrome house. After my dog dies she becomes my password.

When my girlfriend Wynee cries, she really cries. She is crying hysterically in front of the dining hall at Shadow Lake camp because I am leaving early. This is when I figure out how to calm her down. I hug her and begin to whisper the names of our favourite Korean foods in her ear: kimchee, bibimbap, bulgogi, japchae, dduk bokki, seafood pancakes.

I am with my girlfriend Wynee and I am just out of the First Psychosis ward at the psychiatric hospital. Glenn, Wynee's stepfather, says, "Why do you need pot when you have Wynee?" So I quit pot, not that day but soon after. And it's like a fog clears and I feel sane. Wynee's smile, and her laugh, and her love of perfume, and her love of makeup, and her breasts, which she lets me touch and kiss. She takes a long time to get dressed. I am patient. She is so beautiful.

I become spoken word poet M.C. Rymdikulous when I'm fifteen. It starts with a line from a poem by W.B. Yeats. I like the line about "tread softly, for you tread on my dreams," so I borrow it for my own poem.

Regrets

Why was I brought into love,
was it to experience ups and downs?
To me, I believe, it was to express myself freely
or to encounter emotional feelings.
To fall asleep and open yourself up to dreams,
while the one you love treads softly upon
your dreams, love pours out into streams.
How do you know when love is true?
or do you just know it's true
when you do, meet the one you love.
Don't let beauty blind you,
because outside reflection
does not compare to the inner perfection.
The world is full of mistakes
made by the human race,
and yet hope is triggered when you enter open gates,
then you would debate,
do whatever it takes—
Should you date?
Is it safe to say
your life is full of regrets?
Emotional debts, dares and bets?
I don't know if love is true,
but when I do,
love is still yet to come.

My favourite rappers:

Tupac.
K'naan. I once hear him live at the Phoenix and everyone sings along to all of his songs, including Wavin' Flag.
K-OS. He used to live on my street.
Wyclef.
Common.
Jay-Z.
Biggie. I am big, too.
Kardinal.
Dizzee Rascal.
St. Lunatics.
Dre.
Outkast.
Ludakris.
Snoop Dogg.
Drake.
The Fugees.

My favourite blues singers:

Etta James.
Keb Mo.
Johnny Lang.
Lightnin' Hopkins.
B.B. King.
Muddy Waters.
Taj Mahal. We see him once at Harbourfront and he sees my fedora and says, "Cool lid, man."
And my favourite singer of all time: Janis Joplin, because I like her raspy voice. We drive around with the windows down singing "Piece of My Heart" at the top of our lungs, and then singing "Summertime."

I like to play with language the way I dive through the water.

I'm twelve and my mom is making cake at the cottage, but needs something to stir the mix with. She gets a stick from the beach. and I tell her if she uses the stick she'll be making a "dirty sticky lakey smelly cake." But I eat it anyway, even if she stirred it with the beach stick.

I am coming upstairs to the kitchen when I'm fourteen: "Good morning, parents from a distant planet."

When my mom hands me a homemade latte, I ask, "Has it been syruped and stirred?"

My mom gives me a Nespresso machine for my twenty-fifth birthday. All the flavours have names like Stormio and Odacio and Intenso, and they have ratings for how strong they are. One morning I say to my dad, "Did you hear about the new Nespresso flavour? It's called Pinocchio. It says it's a seven but it's more like a four." My dad is laughing so hard he almost slides down to the floor.

Sometimes you need new words to say things.

When I'm seven I come up from the Jewish Community Centre locker room with my shoes untied. I explain to my parents that "my socks got shrinkled."

I'm nine, and my dad, who's always in a hurry, is trying to get me out the door to get to school. I say: "Aren't you a little rushy-pushy?"

My dad and I take a long bike ride, all the way down to the ferry boat and back and forth on the Toronto Islands to fish the ponds and canals, and then all the way back up to St. Clair West. I haven't ridden so far in a long time and my *tuches* and legs are pretty sore. "Tomorrow will be a walking-leg-spreadable day," I say.

One day I'm swimming at the Jewish Community Centre and I remember a poem I heard Lemon do that night in New York, and I start to make up my own version of it. I tell my dad to get some paper and a pen, so he gets out of the pool and borrows paper and pen from the lifeguard. Each length I do I am saying the rhymes in my head, and then I surface at the end of the lane and dictate the poem to my dad. He keeps running from one end of the pool to the other, and I get a good swim in because it's a long poem. He says it may be the first time in history a poem was written underwater. It is dedicated to Lemon. It is about love, of course.

Me without You
is a witch without her cult
a bank without its vault
the dead sea without its salt
Me without You
is a scotsman without his kilt
a jew without his guilt
schwarzenegger without his build
a granny without her quilt
Me without You
is a fisherman without a bite
the sky without its light
Me without You
is a sandwich without its bun
a convent without a nun
a father without a son
Me without You
is a singer without a song
an older brother without his bong
Me without You
is a dog without a tongue
a mermaid without a lung
Me without You
is arabia without its oil
free land without its soil

an egg without its boil
Me without You
is cleaning without a broom
a bride without a groom
an egyptian without a tomb
Me without You
is the evening without its dusk
an elephant without its tusk
a man without his musk
Me without You
is soup without its broth
a punk without a goth
Me without You
is a poem without a rhyme
a margarita without a lime
the swamp without its slime
a dealer without his dime
Me without You
is an owl without its hoot
a tree without its fruit
a pirate without his loot
a mensch without his suit
Me without You
is a flag without its mast
a life without a past
a movie without a cast
experience without a blast
What would You be,
You without Me?

I'm on the couch when my dog Jewelz comes back from a walk. I notice right away there's something different about her. She doesn't come over to lick me. My dad says she never even stopped to pee on their walk, after she'd lunged at something in the alleyway—but it was dark and he didn't see if she picked up anything. My dog always comes over for lickies, so I know something is going on. I grab her and force her mouth open and sure enough there's something in it: a rotten old chicken bone she scavenged. She looked so innocent when she came in, but that was the giveaway. I have Prader-Willi Syndrome, and I'm really good at hiding stolen food, so I recognize her expression right away. I take the rotten bone away and give it to my dad, who laughs.

My first dog was a border collie named Mishigas. Jewelz is my second dog. Soft brown eyes. Sharp pointy ears. I chose her name. My dad always says she is an importunate dog who always wants our attention. I like to be importuned by my dog. I let her sleep with me. I let her kiss me. It is good to be loved so much, and to love her back, even if she can be a *noodge* sometimes. We take her to the dog park in Cedarvale Ravine and I stand at one end and my dad climbs the hill at the other end. Then I call Jewelz and she runs straight to me, and then my dad does his big whistle and she runs across the field and up the hill to him. That must be the part of her that is a border collie. She likes to know where everyone is. We train Jewelz to walk along the top of the fence at the dog park at Hillcrest Park. All the other dog owners are very impressed. But Mishigas could do more tricks because she was a pure-bred border collie. We believe the purpose of training our dog is to make the other dog owners ask, "How did you train her to do that?"

My dog Jewelz licks my face. My dad says, "Ewww!" and makes a face, but my girlfriend lives in Sutton and I don't see her very often, and anyway a kiss is a kiss. My beautiful dog, who we chose as a puppy up at a farm north of Guelph on a winter's day, and who I named "Jewelz," with a "z", in case anyone asks how to spell it. My dad and my dog wait for me at the corner of Winona and St. Clair after my morning shift. When I see them I drop down and do a sort of knees-bent-squat-waddle towards Jewelz, and she wags her tail so hard it looks like her *tuches* will fall off. Then she jumps up to lick my face, and I have to move my headphones away or she will knock them off. They are there waiting for me every day.

I take many photos of Jewelz. Jewelz jumping the fence. Jewelz running at Hillcrest dog park. Jewelz swimming in the lake at Cherry Beach. My favourite Jewelz photo is when she is splashing through the water and it looks like she has little, white waterwings like an angel from all the spray and foam she makes jumping and swimming.

My dad and I pack our fishing gear and take the subway down to Ontario Place. We read somewhere that there's good fishing down in the marina. But what we don't realize is that the place is closed for construction or something. It feels like a ghost town. So we sneak past the security booth with our fishing gear. We call it "doing a Romanian," because Romanians—like my grandmother—like to break rules. We sneak in and find a pond full of fish and start fishing in the marinas and lagoons and the channels they use for paddleboats. Then we wander closer to the lake and find a pond full of fish, and we see an otter. There is a sunken freighter that acts as a breakwater. And there's a high tower with a cabin for the harbourmaster, and we climb up. There's a huge carp skeleton picked clean. There's a sign on the door: ABSOLUTELY NO ADMITTANCE. My dad and I try the door and it's unlocked, so we go in. It's empty in the harbourmaster's cabin, so the best part of climbing up to it was opening a door that says ABSOLUTELY NO ADMITTANCE. No one catches us that day and we wander through the whole place feeling like spies.

When we go back later that summer the security cops throw us out. Even my dad's smooth-talking doesn't work. They escort us right to the entrance. On our third visit we go just inside and find an abandoned marina and my dad catches a huge pike and then I catch a huge largemouth bass. Catch. Shoot photo. Release. Catch. Shoot. Release.

I make pearl necklaces. There are no shortcuts for pearl-knotting. But sometimes, no matter how careful I am, I knot the whole necklace and get to the clasp, and the silk thread breaks, and I have to cut the necklace apart and start again. I used to get so discouraged when this happened, but then I learned to just keep going and make it again. Whenever I make a necklace I show it to my mom and dad, and we admire the lustre of the pearls. Their nacre. Mostly my necklaces sell for $200–$400. Whenever I sell one at a craft fair I am so happy. Then I go out and buy more pearls to make more necklaces. I keep them all in a rolling bead case with many drawers. My dad calls it Ali Baba's cave, and I know that story, and how Ali Baba finds a treasure and takes it from the forty thieves. He told it to me when I was five, and I still remember how Ali Baba's brother Cassim gets chopped into little pieces by the robbers after he tried to cheat Ali Baba.

This is what I do to make pearl necklaces:

Step by step:

- Cut loose all pearls from strand;
- Select proper thickness of silk and colour;
- Remove silk from card and stretch;
- Make a knot at the end of stretched silk thread;
- Thread needle of thread through knot cover;
- Slide knot cover to very end of silk thread and cover knot;
- Thread all the pearls;
- Hand-knot every pearl to complete pearl necklace;
- Thread needle of thread through second knot cover;
- Make knot;
- Close knot covers;
- Attach clasp.

I'm seventeen and in my second high school, and I mess up at West Toronto and get suspended and write a letter apologizing. I have to write these letters every once in a while, wherever I'm going to school or camp.

Dear School,

Last week I put not only myself but other people in a non-safe environment. And no, I haven't acted or displayed features of a good role model for grade nines or others. I'm very sorry about this, and I will try to do this in future. What I did was wrong, stupid, and regrettable, and I feel that in some way I have a debt to pay back to you all as a school. West Toronto isn't just a school, it's a community of laughter, concentration, and learning, and because of my actions I have betrayed the school's communityism. I would love to give back to this school some of my time to form with assistance two clubs. One club for people who share my interest in fishing (where we could go out and fish together as an extracurricular activity). And second, a club to play games of a challenging nature for those Bogglers, Scrabblers, and soon-to-be-beaten Monopolysts.

I hope to bring this school together as a stronger community. And I will step forth into this school once again, but as someone with positive intentions to commit to this school to the best of my abilities. With these last words I want to apologize for my drinking and to assure you this won't happen again, but also to say that nobody is perfect.

Sincerely,

Jacob Zavitz

I am seventeen when I write this poem.

I'll be there by spirit
I'll be there beside you while my body is gone
My soul is your companion touching you spiritually
While I'm gone
It might feel I'm light years away
But every day
I will wander close to you
My absence will make loneliness wander
But also will make the heart more tender.

We are always teasing each other. On a Monday morning my dad is trying to get me to wake up. He says, "I'm trying to access www.jacob.ca." I answer, "Connection failure." I'm eighteen, almost nineteen, and moving slowly in the morning, and I tell him: "I'm almost ready to start getting ready."

And one day, no teasing, I'm walking with my dad and dog to work in the morning and tell him: "I love my life!" And I do, because I have changed so much, and I have a girlfriend, and I have a best friend, and I have become an excellent photographer, and I make jewellery, and I love my neighbourhood, and I have my own fishing kayak and great gear, and I have a job, and I have a sweet dog, and I know that my brother and mother and dad love me.

Mom and I like to watch TV. We binge-watch shows on Netflix. I go to her place every Monday night for supper and television. We watch every episode of *NCIS* and *How I Met Your Mother* and *Big Bang Theory*. We don't watch sci-fi even though she likes it, but I can't stand it. I like crime and comedy. I watch *Sons of Anarchy* and *The Sopranos* on my own because they are too violent for her. It is good to watch all the episodes of your favourite shows snuggled on a couch with someone you love. My dad picks me up after the last episode and we drive home. My dad doesn't know how to veg out, but my mom and I are really good at it. She is excellent at hugging me. She is the best hugger.

When I'm seven I am trying to see the full moon but my mom is in the way. I tell her, "You're blocking the view." She says, "I am the view!"

And when I'm eight I'm trying to do my homework but it's hard and I tell her, "Mommy, I just got mixed up." She's so calm. She says, "Well, unmix yourself, dear." My dad would have started telling me stuff like "I should have been prepared blah blah blah etc. etc.'" but my mom doesn't get flustered. They are very different kinds of people.

I'm thirteen and my mom is at the breakfast table looking dishevelled. I say to my dad: "You picked the most gruesomest woman ever to have babies with." She laughs because she knows I think she is really beautiful.

When I'm eighteen my parents are mad at each other, sulking and simmering but never lifting their voices. "Since you can't yell at Mom," I tell my dad, "why don't you send her a text in caps?"

I make jewellery. Mom weaves, quilts, and knits scarves, and grows flowers, and wears my jewellery. She and I love patterns. And we have lots of patience when we are making things. I give her many pearl necklaces, and she gives me gemstones.

I am twenty and she comes back from her trip to Holland with a huge piece of labradorite. It's too big to make into a piece of jewellery, but I love to hold it and look at it.

She and I also love gadgets. She always has the latest i-whatever, and I'm always shopping at Henry's Camera store for new stuff.

We both love to make beauty. My mom takes up knitting and the first thing she makes is a neckwarmer for me and a neckwarmer for my brother. When she drops a stitch she curses. A lot. Which is funny because knitting is such a quiet thing to do. I wear my neckwarmer all the time. It's a warm rust colour, with soft wool. One day I go fishing at Leslie Spit, and we have to ride our bikes pretty far to get to a good fishing spot. I forget my neckwarmer out on some rocks, and don't remember until I get all the way home. The next day we ride back. It's a really long bike ride. But it's worth it because we find the neckwarmer. Every time I wear it I feel hugged.

My semi-precious gemstones:

Turquoise.
Amethyst.
Garnet.
Tiger-eye.
Agate.
Amber.
Onyx.
Hematite.
Rutilated Quartz.
Sesame Jasper.
Aquamarine.
Citrine.
Labradorite.
Pearls of every size and shape.
Red Abalone.
Blue Abalone.
Tourmaline.
Peridot.

We are in the V-stern canoe we used before I got my Hobie Pro Angler. We have a Torqueedo electric motor on the stern. I am twenty-one and my parents are splitting up, but my dad still comes to the cottage that summer so we can fish one more time on Roddick Lake. We are heading to Lac des Pères, which connects to Roddick through a little rapids that used to have a portage trail alongside. No one fishes Lac des Pères and I really want to wet a line there. The trail used to be open to anyone who wanted to walk it, but then somebody bought it and put up a sign: PRIVÉ. We hate the sign, but now we meet the owner—Gérard—and he's nice. He invites us in for a beer, and shows us how he built the cottage himself, and then says we can hike the trail and try our luck. We leave the boat tied up at his dock. It's early evening, and rain is coming. My dad and I hurry along the trail and come out on the big rocks at the other end, and I start casting for bass. Even though it's drizzling, it's fun to fish a fresh lake. My dad keeps looking at the light and says that we have to go because he doesn't want to be caught out on the lake after dark. Thing is, it's hard to stop fishing. I'm catching smallmouth bass, and tossing them back in, and they're really big. So by the time we get back to our lake and launch our canoe and wave good-bye to Gérard, it's dark and the rain is coming down hard. I shine the flashlight ahead, and my dad starts the electric motor and we head back down the lake. He goes slow because he's worried there's not enough juice in the battery. We are soaked all the way through by now, and only halfway home. I'm not too worried because the smallies were so much fun to catch; but I am relieved when we come around the last point and see the lights of our cottage ahead. The battery lasts just till we get to the beach, and we pull the boat up. My dad collects the gear and we walk up the path to the cottage. We stand in the mud room by the front door and start to take off our clothes.

The strange thing is nobody in the livingroom looks up or asks how we are. Mom is reading. Hans and Pearl, who are visiting from Holland, are reading. There's a fire in the stove. It is cozy. But it feels like we had just been in danger, and nobody is worried about us. We take hot showers and put on dry clothes. We think they will greet us like heroes, but they don't. We stop going to that cottage after Frans sells it, but I keep dreaming about fishing that lake where no one else goes: Lac des Pères. I wish there were no signs anywhere that say: PRIVÉ.

We are in Ithaca visiting an antique store, and I see something beautiful. A whole string of cherry amber beads. So beautiful and so rare. I buy them and bring them back to my studio, and then life gets pretty chaotic for a few years and I forget about them. And then, when I try to find them, I can't. They are lost. I look everywhere but they have simply vanished. Years pass and they stay lost. And I can't believe I could lose something so precious to me. But I did.

Then one day my dad and I are cleaning out my room. I am moving from my childhood bedroom to the big room downstairs that was my parents' bedroom before they stopped living together. There is an IKEA dresser I don't want anymore, and we start to roll it out of the room so my dad can put it out in front of the house so someone can take it. One of the drawers slides open as we tilt it. There is an envelope stuck to the back of the drawer. I open it and there is my string of cherry amber beads. We had almost put them out on the curb. If the drawer hadn't slid open at just that angle I would never have found them and some total stranger would discover my precious cherry amber. I must have hidden them there because I was afraid of them being stolen. Then I forgot.

It is so easy to forget the things that are valuable, and then to lose them forever. I begin planning the special necklace I will make with the cherry amber. I will give it to my mom.

We are driving home from Ithaca where we had visited our friends Jonathan and Mary Alyce. We celebrate the Fourth of July and now we're on the New York State Thruway heading home and there's a farmers' market outside one of the rest stations. We buy a bag of cherries for the road and are munching them on the patio. An African-American man comes out with his wife, and sees us eating the cherries, and asks us, "They sweet, they good?" And we tell him yes, they sweet, they good. And from then on we always say "they sweet they good" whenever life is going well.

My dad is running the Toronto Storytelling Festival in 2014. He has an image for the festival but he asks my advice for how to make it better. The image shows seven animals sitting around a fire, with the city of Toronto skyline in the background. They must be on one of the Toronto Islands, maybe even the secret spot my dad and go to when we are fishing over there. The animals are Bear, Snake, Spider, Coyote, Raven, Turtle, Rabbit. It is sunset. They are all looking at the fire. I tell him, "Ask the artist to make the coyote turn towards us." The artist changes the picture, and now the coyote is looking out of the circle around the fire, and is looking towards us, and that changes everything. We are part of the magic circle. I like the way the coyote looks towards us as we look towards him and the others. They each have lots of stories told about them: Bear, Spider, Coyote, Turtle, Raven, Rabbit, Snake. The coyote looking out makes us part of their story.

I am twenty-three and I'm wearing my hospital gown and walking with my dad on College Street. I'm about to get discharged from the Centre for Addiction and Mental Health, where I've been living for three weeks getting treatment for psychosis for my second time. I didn't have to wear the gown, but I did. A few years before that, getting a sleep test for apnea, I even went to the Tim Hortons donut shop near Toronto Western Hospital and I was still wearing all the electrodes. I pretended to be a zombie. It was a good time watching people in the donut shop stare.

Today we are on our way to the Starbucks at College and St. George, and we see a couple standing at the corner reading a map. My dad walks up to them and asks if they need help. He and I like to talk to strangers. Her name is Judith and his name is Göksen (he has to teach me how to say it). They say they are trying to get to a campground by the Rouge River, on the east side of town. My dad and I are puzzled. Who goes camping in Toronto? They each have huge, serious-looking backpacks. They say they've just flown in from Iceland, where they'd been hiking in the glaciers, and they were from Hamburg, Germany, and they were travelling the world.

My dad turns to me and whispers, "Should we ask them to visit? They could camp in the backyard." "Okay," I say. So he tells them that when they are done camping by the Rouge River they can camp in our yard, near Bathurst and St. Clair. He gives them his cell number and we all say goodbye and they go to the subway on their way out to Scarborough. Two days later, Judith calls and asks if it is still okay for them to come to our place. My dad says yes.

When I come out of the hospital and come home, Judith and Göksen are there and then they stay for four months. They pitch their tent in the livingroom when the weather turns cold, and then they move into my dad's study. They are nice to be with except when they are bickering. They eventually leave to travel the world, and when they get back to Germany they break up. Judith falls in love with an Icelandic sheep farmer, and has a baby. Göksen moves to Berlin. He was a Turkish-German, and knew how to read the future in coffee grounds from Turkish coffee.

But I never let him read mine.

These are some of my favourite places:

Bouchette, Quebec, where the cottage is.
Amsterdam and Aerdenhout and Heemstede in Holland.
London, England.
Ithaca and New York City.
Letchworth State Park south of Buffalo and Covewood Lodge in the Adirondacks.
Pittsburgh.
Detroit.
Santa Barbara and Los Angeles.
Montreal.
Camp Couchiching, Camp Kennebec, Camp Concord.
Shadow Lake near Stouffville, Ontario.
Ottawa and Maniwaki.
Buffalo and Rochester.
Crow Lake.
Devil's Lake.
Lake Nosbonsing.
Toronto Islands.
Leslie Spit.
Ontario Place.
Poplar Hill, Ontario.
St. Clair West, my neighbourhood.

I have to wait a long time to shoot the hawk framed in a triangle of branches at the edge of the gorge at Letchworth State Park in New York. I wait and wait and wait for the hawk to appear at the exact spot between the branches.

I'm twenty-three, and my dad had made up a bag of cheese for me, but I sneak it out of his bag before he has a chance to give it to me. When he's surprised it's not there, I tell him, "It got Jaked." It's a Prader-Willi Syndrome joke. People like me are really good at sneaking food from counters, bags, garbage bins, and other people's lunches.

One night we go next door for a visit with Sean and Myriam. I like to go over and sing "Jolene" with them. Sean and I really belt it out, especially if we've had a few drinks. They have a niece with Prader-Willi Syndrome, and know about keeping food locked up. But when I go downstairs to pee, I see there is a fridge, so naturally I have to investigate. In the freezer is a container with the word PEPPERMINT written on it. It sure looks like a box of chocolate, so I take it out and open it. My mouth is watering.

But inside the box is a dead, frozen, shrivelled-up hamster. I go back upstairs and confess that I tried to raid their fridge but instead of finding chocolate I found a freeze-dried hamster. They tell me it's from when their kids were little and they lived on Crawford St., and when their hamster died they didn't have the heart to bury it but couldn't figure out what else to do with it. So they just kept it in their freezer. For years. The hamster's name was PEPPERMINT.

It's Passover, and I'm twenty-three. I'm crying because my dad got chopped liver with egg from Nortown Deli instead of chopped liver without egg. Everyone in my family likes chopped liver without egg, and my dad only got chopped liver with egg because they were sold out of chopped liver without egg. People with Prader-Willi Syndrome take our food pretty seriously. Food can make us happy, and food can make us cry.

My favourite foods:

Dumplings, fried and steamed but fried is better.
Rotis.
Buns, all kinds.
Barbeque chicken sandwiches from Churrasco—these are huge, and I've only had them a couple of times.
Filipino stuffed somethings.
Rice balls from the Italian butcher, who doesn't smile very often.
Muffins.
Cheese.
Festivals from Gerry's Jamaican.
Doubles.
Frozen grapes.
Yvette calls me "polpetto"—dumpling—when I am three years old at Sprouts daycare.
Ice cream.
Lisa's carrot cake.
Pizza from Da Maria.
Pasta, especially tortellini.
But there's something I hate. When I'm eight my dad cooks mushroom-flavoured risotto. I can't eat it. There's not much I won't eat, but this is really awful. I say: "They smell like socks and taste like shoes."

When I'm twenty-four my dad forgets the key to the fridge on the kitchen table, and I really enjoy eating all the cheese and all the peanut butter. Then I leave a note with a riddle for my dad.

I have a neck
If I could walk, I would have four legs
I can open doors
That would be dangerous … to One.
Who am I?
Where am I?
Why haven't I been secured?

I hear him when he reads it. He yells, "Shit!" when he realizes what the riddle was about. Then he laughs and locks everything up again.

Another time he forgets to put the food away and I leave another note.

"Someone has looked at us with threatening eyes. Can anyone protect us? Sincerely, Boiled Eggs."

I hear him laugh and then say sorry.

Life with Prader-Willi Syndrome is dramatic.

On a walkabout near the Miles Nadal Jewish Community Centre, I see a pair of well-worn boots tied together and left on the sidewalk by Bloor and Spadina. You can see they are made of good leather. They are quality boots, but now they have been left behind. And I take a photo because I wonder who left them there. Where have they travelled? Will someone find them and wear them again? And to go with the photo, I write: The mile walked by someone who left their shoes behind is far longer than the mile walked by someone with their shoes on. My dad shows the photo sometimes to the psychiatry patients he tells stories with at Baycrest. They tell him things like: "We know what those shoes feel like."

I am a twenty-five-year-old crossing guard. Leeann Moore is my support worker. She helps me before and after my shifts. One day she is walking my dog back from the intersection where I'm still working, and they are walking back along St. Clair. She is in front of the Salvation Army just east of Christie Street. A woman parks and begins to unload stuff, and her dog jumps out and attacks Jewelz. Her dog is vicious and goes right for my dog's throat. If I'd've been there I would've fuckin' killed the other dog. I start to shake with rage when Leeann tells me afterwards what happened. The owner stands there and doesn't know how to stop her dog from attacking my dog, and Leeann yells at her and the woman says, "I forgot to put his muzzle on!" and then Leeann, who is fearless, grabs the vicious dog by the jaws and rips it away from Jewelz, and screams at the woman to get the leash and get the dog under control. Leeann uses her bare hands to pull the crazy dog off my dog and holds the huge dog's jaws shut while it growls and keeps trying to attack. The woman finally gets her dog back in the car, and says she'll pay our vet bill, and sure enough Jewelz is bleeding and it costs about $800 to have her wound stitched up. When Leeann tells me this story I ask her how she had the courage to do it, and she says she did it because it had to be done, like it was no big thing. Leeann is so brave. Jackie Moore, Leeann's sister, was my support worker, too, plus Malka, Dan, Steve, Jaron, Rachel, Travis, Lucy, Mark, Arlene in grade eight. I am lucky I have such good support workers even though it takes me a long time to admit I need help. I'm lucky one of them isn't afraid of vicious dogs, and that none of them is afraid of Prader-Willi Syndrome.

We befriend Navid just after he moves to Toronto to marry his girlfriend. He is from London, and has a chow. We see him a lot in the neighbourhood. One day he tells us what happened when he walked with his dog in the Cedarvale dog park. Another dog attacked them, and bit Navid on the arm. They called the police. The couple who owned the vicious dog didn't apologize, and the woman started to yell at Navid, and then an old guy nearby told him he should move back to where he came from and Navid laughed and said, "You mean England?" and the whole thing got really ugly, and the woman was screaming racist things at him, and then he said to the vicious woman with her vicious dog, "Pipe down, love." He sues the woman and she has to pay $12,000. She should have piped down.

My record at planking is one minute and fifteen seconds. My trainer Phil makes me jog, plank, spin, lift medicine balls, do squats, haul a sledge. My dad comes near the end and watches. Sometimes he takes a video, which he sends to my mom and my brother. He says it's the best show in town. My shirt is soaked from the workout, and my face is red. Then we walk over to Harry's health food store and I get a cold kombucha. Phil's fitness studio is called Philosophy Fitness, and I get the joke a long time before my dad does. Phil. Philosophy. He tells me I'm his "project" and I can see that I am getting stronger because I go there.

Alan Shain is the second person I know who has cerebral palsy. He's a standup comedian who once fell off the stage the only time he actually tried to stand up doing standup. We love each other. I even give him my black leather jacket, which makes me look like Elvis, especially when I curl my lip like Elvis. When I am in the hospital in Pittsburgh on a locked Prader-Willi Syndrome ward, Alan sends me a joke book with a picture of Groucho Marx on the cover. It helps me survive a place I hate.

My roommate George weighs 500 pounds and needs a special bed. He is the fattest person I've ever met, and has the best chuckle ever. I am afraid I'll become as big as George.

Effie, my best friend, has cerebral palsy too. She is fearless. She travels through Canada by herself taking photos. She hosts game nights at her apartment in Scarborough. I teach Effie to play Settlers of Catan and she teaches me to play poker. Sometimes her friends come to her place in Scarborough, and we all play Cards Against Humanity and drink lots of Appleton rum, and I am so happy. It is the first time in my life that I have a group of friends. We all have something or other—cerebral palsy, Prader-Willi Syndrome, whatever—but we are just pals together drinking and laughing, and everyone—mostly—likes my dirty jokes and we laugh and laugh.

Lisa runs World Class Bakers at Christie and St. Clair West. She is my friend. She is a little gruff and doesn't smile much, but she always smiles for me. And she watched over me when I was going through psychosis, and was wandering through the streets to find dealers. People don't know this about her, but I would often see Lisa sending giant pots of soup over to the church across the street to feed homeless people. She never told people she was doing this, but I noticed. So when someone posts a nasty comment about Lisa, I tell the neighbourhood the truth about her, and how warm and generous she is. I love Lisa, and especially her homemade carrot cake with thick icing. She's one of the neighbourhood eccentrics. I know all of them.

Stephen, the Jamaican guy who washes windows and quotes scripture.

Gladys, who I give cigarettes to. She is scary-looking and most people hurry by her, but I know she is gentle and I tease her by saying, "Don't work too hard," and she always answers, "I never do." Her fingernails are very long, and she looks like a witch, but she likes that I know her name and give her smokes. She disappears one day.

Mohamed wears funny hats. He walks with his head tilted to one side and always has a cigarette in his mouth and never bends his arm down when he takes the cigarette in and out of his mouth. It's like he's saluting to some invisible officer. We think he was in a war in the Horn of Africa and maybe got shell-shocked. I always greet him by saying "Salaam Aleikum" and he answers, "Aleikum Salaam." I don't know his story, even though I see him every day sitting in front of McDonald's.

There's a guy who wears a cap with bull horns on it. He seems normal except that he impersonates a toro as he walks along St. Clair.

There is a church at the corner of Wychwood and St. Clair which has been closed for years. A homeless person makes a kind of a nest on a side porch, with cardboard walls. I send a photo to the St. Clair West Facebook group to let people know this person needed a mattress and blankets.

And Stavros is a man in the neighbourhood who had his leg amputated for some reason. For a long time I watch him in a wheelchair on Christie Street, rolling himself along, kicking himself forward with his one leg. Then one day I see that he is finally walking with an artificial leg, and I say, "You're doing really well now!" and he smiles so much. He tells my dad that I am the only person in the neighbourhood who noticed that he was walking again, and praised him for it. One or two words can change everything.

My dad's phone has an alarm set for 6:30 am. That's when he gets up to prepare breakfast so we can then walk over to my first shift, stopping for an espresso along the way. I type a message for him, which shows up with the alarm from Monday to Friday. I write: "Wake the fuck up, every weekday."

Each weekday morning on my way to work we I go to Krave café on St. Clair. We step up to the counter and say, "The usual, please." Because we come every day, they know that the "usual" means a single espresso for my dad and a double espresso for me, though they only charge for a single. Sometimes we tease the staff and instead of saying the "usual" we say the "recurrent." Or we make it fancy and my dad says we'll have the "quotidian." If Beth-Ann and her daughter Georgia are there we tease each other about which Norse god the weekday is named after. Thursday is named after Thor. Wednesday is named after Odin. Friday is named after someone called Freya. My dad knows all this stuff from being a storyteller. Then we walk together to my intersection and I work the morning shift while my dad takes our dog to Hillcrest Park. And this is what happens every weekday morning at 7:45 am. The usual.

I see a mural of a bird near the Jewish Community Centre: red and yellow door, blue and white bird feathers. I use my fisheye lens so the bird curves around and you can't really tell what you're seeing except that I leave a little corner of sky in the upper-left edge of the photo so you can get some perspective. I use a fish-eye to capture the bird's-eye looking at us, with our human eyes.

Valerie and I get along—mostly. She comes twice a month to clean our house, and she is also a friend. Once when I had the crazies I said something mean, and she was insulted, and stopped speaking to me. She'd come to work without even looking at me. But I was mad, too, and wouldn't apologize. But then I did, and she forgave me. I like the way she speaks Jamaican patois. My dad always makes her hardboiled eggs, which she calls "heggs," and she does really love me despite me hurting her feelings that time. She knew me from the time I was born. She once said to my dog Mishigas, "Stop looking at me in that tone of eyes."

I love her, too, and after she got sick and couldn't work for us anymore, I would go see her sometimes and neither one of us ever remembers why we both got so mad all those years back.

I stand at the intersection with my whistle and stop sign. The drivers sometimes get mad at me. They say stuff with their windows closed. Sometimes they try to sneak through their left turns and their right turns even with children in the intersection. I yell at them and tell them it's my job to keep their children safe. But they just want to get to work a minute faster. My friend David is also a crossing guard, and sometimes we blow our whistles at each other on St. Clair, and then we stop and talk about how stupid drivers are. Don't they know I'm protecting the children?

I try not to let them hurt my feelings, but it's hard. Sometimes the constable sends me new crossing guards to train, which is how I know he thinks I'm doing a good job. When a driver has really gotten to me, I tell my dad, and he reminds me what my Grandpa Jack from Detroit would say: "Fuck 'em." It's a useful saying.

The parents of the kids I cross at Winona and Benson give me so many gift cards: Starbucks, Cineplex, Indigo, Krave Cafe, Tim Hortons. I get them at Christmas and at the end of the school year. Once a woman parks her car on Benson near Winona and leaves the door unlocked while she goes around to the trunk to get something. She has already unlocked the baby's seatbelt. I see what happens next. The toddler comes out of the back of the car and starts running straight into the intersection looking for her mother. My blood turns to ice. Everything moves so fast and at the same time so slowly. I whistle and scream at the cars, and they all stop just in time. One almost hits the baby but stops just a couple of centimetres away. The driver doesn't see her but stops when he hears my whistle. The mother jumps too and then sees her little girl in the middle of the road so close to the car's bumper, and she runs to her and picks her up and holds her tight and they are both crying. I hear the mother say, "That man saved your life!"

Later, when I tell my dad what happened, I cry too. And I say, "Maybe that's why I chose to live."

On Saturday mornings I walk over to the farmers' market at the Artscape Wychwood Barns. I dress for the occasion. A mink stole. It's women's clothing but I don't care. In winter, a raccoon fur coat or maybe my lamb fleece coat. In nice weather my cream-coloured sports jacket. I choose one of my forty hats—maybe my Borsalino or Wildhagen—and tilt it at just the right angle. I know I'm the coolest-looking guy on the boulevard and one time the father of one of the kids I cross at my crosswalk sees me in my fancy clothes and says, "Are you a pimp or a crossing guard?"

After walking through the market and visiting all the stalls that have free samples, I go to Ali's Fish Shaq and order a fish roti. It has:

The roti wrap.
Potatoes mixed with vegetables.
Fried plantains.
Avocado.
Sprouts.
Pickled peppers and onions.
Hot sauce made from Scotch bonnet peppers and papaya.
Fried butterfish.

And then I have Ali put in their homemade coconut drops, which are sweet. It's my own invention. It's one mighty roti. They call it "The Jacob." I may be the only person in the world with a roti named after him.

The farmers' market is my favourite place to be on a Saturday morning. All of the farmers know me. I take my roti to where my mother is sitting, or sometimes to the storytelling tent where my dad usually goes. When my dad sees me arrive, with a roti in my hand and my cool hat, his eyes shine with pride at his good-looking son. Sometimes he is wearing his own brown fedora from Big It Up.

My hats:

Borsalino.
Stetson.
Big It Up.
Sammy Taft.
Magill.
Top hats.
Bowlers.
Fedoras, more than 30 of them.
A Bolero.
Legends League. My brother gives me two cool Legends League caps. I have a button that says "MY OTHER LIFE IS PERFECT." I pin it on one of my caps.
Pork pies.
Wildhagens, handmade on Queen Street.
Goorin Brothers.
I collect hats at King of Kensington and Caravan and Cabaret where my friend Tao worked and he is always nice to me even in my crazy years.
Dobbs.
Birkdales.
Biltmore.
Buttini.
Huthauser Sedlarik.
Fléchet.
Scala.
Elks.

The belly dancers are performing on Augusta Avenue one summer afternoon in Kensington Market. There are no cars allowed, so they are dancing in the street with a sound system. I like the way they move so gracefully. I like that the leader has a big tummy like me, and moves so freely. She is beautiful. I don't ask for their permission as I shoot but afterwards I show them the photos and they like them. So many naked, beautiful women's bellies shaking and moving. My dad whispers something: "Must be jelly, jam don't shake like that!" He's from Detroit, and they say stuff like that, or they used to.

We call the stuff I say Jacobisms and my dad writes them down in his Book of Quotes. They become family proverbs.

When I'm five I tell my parents: "Don't you love the world!"

And when I'm six I tell them: "Your son Jacob is not an ordinary person."

And I am six and a half when I tell my parents, "You should call me 'beautiful sunshine.'" And they do, until they come up with a different nickname.

My dad likes to sing a silly song over and over again: "Oh dear, what can the matter be? Seven old ladies got locked in the lavatory …" I'm eight years old and change it to: "Oh dear, what can the matter be? Seven old ladies got trapped in the melody."

My friend Stephen is over on a sleepover. We're eight and a half. He wants to talk but it's late, so I tell him, "I'm tired. I already gave my mouth a big workout today."

We're at the locker room at the Jewish Community Centre and I say, "Hey, Dad, did you know you have more hair on your ass than on your chest?" We've been coming here all my life and I know all the *alterkackers*.

One weekend I forget to set my clock after Daylight Saving Time and I text my mom: "Hey I'm living in two different time zones. My room is 11:24 and upstairs is 10:24. Is my room its own country? Can I have my own government? Or am I just a piece of a continent?"

I am fourteen and go to my first semi-formal and come home and say: "I grinded with the school president!"

I'm fourteen and at our family doctor and she tells me I need to be tested for glasses. I'm trying to read the numbers on a clock, and I can't. So I say, "How can I read them? They're green and blurry."

I am seventeen and say, "I like to think people my age wait until there are no more clothes before they do their laundry." And then, same age and carrying too many secrets, I tell my parents, "My whole life is encrypted."

When I watch a movie called *Bangkok Dangerous* I tell my dad, "It was hold-you-in-your-place kind of slow."

I am twenty, drinking my morning coffee with my parents. I tell them, "With every sip you all become more bearable."

When I am twenty-six, I'm talking to my dad. "Can you predict tomorrow?" I ask. "Um ... like Travis coming to do support work ...?" "Can you predict tomorrow?" I ask again. "No." "Then enjoy today!" I am way better at enjoying today than my dad. He worries about everything all the time. He says a Jewish pessimist is someone who says, "Things can't get any worse," and a Jewish optimist says, "Yes they can."

I am twenty-five and in the hospital again. My parents are with me. We seem to spend a lot of time in emergency rooms. I am wearing nothing but a hospital gown and I say, "If this was strip poker, I'd be winning." We all laugh and laugh, even here. My family is a teasing family. When I have the crazies my parents tease each other in the emergency room at the mental hospital, though I am strapped down and raving and they had already split up.

They tease after my operation for Fournier's gangrene. They tease whenever we have to go to emergency for the boils I'd get in a delicate part of my anatomy. They tease in the office of my endocrinologist.

Joking helps in hard times. When I'm disappointed that my mom won't be taking me to her friend's wedding, I tell her I am going to be "your negative plus one." One night at a seder my brother is berating me about how much kugel I am taking. When we get to the plagues, somewhere around the locusts, I dip my finger in the wine, drop it on my plate, and say, "Brothers."

My brother Natty's so tough that when he teases me I always laugh.

When he is ten and I am six, Natty is surprised when I offer to help him with his homework. He asks me how I could help him and I tell him, "I helped God when he was little."

He threatens me with a butt-kicking (I'm eight) and I tell him: "My ass is priceless."

I'm eating a carrot and I hiccup and he says, "Carbonated carrot?" Then he makes a comment about my boxers falling down, and I tell him, "Stop picturing my butt in your mind."

I am eating lettuce one day at lunch and we're trying to finish so we can go somewhere, and he says, "When fuckin' Betsy here finishes chewing her chud." But he means "cud," so he gets his comeuppance and we all make fun of him for years and years.

My brother looks at me as we sit together at the table and says, "You have really small eyes." I'm thirteen and I say, "That's so I don't have to look at your ugly face."

At Green Beanery we are having a coffee, and I'm seventeen, and I tell him, "Did I mention I had a rectal examination today?"

I'm twenty and Natty's visiting and my pyjamas slip off my butt. He says, "You're making it hard to feel proud of you right now!"

We are watching my brother direct *Acquainted*, his second movie. I was at the premiere of his first one, *Edging*. I was so proud of him and the whole audience got up at the end and gave him and the crew a standing ovation, and I was shouting and hollering. And it was a nice buffet at the after-party, too.

Now we're at the baseball diamond at Earlscourt Park and there's a whole crew around my brother, and everyone but the actors are wearing headsets and caps and running around preparing the scene. I've never seen my brother be a film director on set before and it is so exciting. They really do say stuff like "Cut!" And what I like so much is to watch everyone show so much respect to him as they get in their positions and get ready for the scene to begin. This is the scene where they're playing baseball in his movie. I don't know anything about baseball, but I am so proud of my brother, and so happy that he is doing what makes him happy. I decide I'll stick to making jewellery and taking photos, which are my way of bringing beauty into the world. Movies are his way.

There are photos I could see but didn't take, and there's one lost photo I wish I could find. My dad and I are walking on the north side of St. Clair after my morning shift. We are walking east towards Christie. The westbound streetcar stop has a long glass barrier, and there are people standing on the other side waiting for the streetcar. It is early winter and the glass hasn't been cleaned for a while, and also it is covered with frost at that hour. The rising sun hits the glass barrier and it becomes even more opaque, which makes it hard to see the real people waiting on the other side, but shows their shadows on the dirty, frosty glass. It feels like seeing ghosts, and not being able to tell if the people are really there. Something like that. We both stop to look at this strange phenomenon. The sun, the glass, the frost, the people waiting, their shadows. We look for it every time we pass there on our walks, but never see it again. And my dad says, "It's amazing what you see when you're out without your gun." Or camera. I call it my lost ghost photo.

There is an alleyway next to Krave, where we go every morning on my way to work. We are walking south towards Benson. My dad says, "I think I just saw something really big fly to the top of that tree." There's a tall pine tree at the end of the alley. "I'm not sure, though, but it may have been a really big bird." There is a breeze and we both see that the whole tree is swaying a bit, but not the very top. Which seems strange. Then, just as we are almost there, we see a huge hawk explode from the top of the tree, pump its wings, and disappear in the direction of Wychwood Park. It's gone in a second. We stand there in awe. I have no camera.

My lost photo is from the time I see an older woman sitting (like the boots) on a sidewalk on St. George just north of Bloor. We are walking to L'Express for brunch. She is nicely dressed, but she is sitting like a street person on the pavement, and she is blowing bubbles with a big plastic ring. And I wonder: why? Bubbles are light and iridescent and happy, and she is smiling as she blows them. But she is sitting there like a panhandler, all alone. I take this picture without her seeing me. My eye is drawn to stray objects, and stray people. I may have deleted it, though, because I can't find it anymore.

Bernard, upstairs, is who I show my stuff to: fedoras, fishing gear, photography equipment. He is my live-in uncle. He is always interested in everything I show him. I tease him about being single. He teases me back. He wears shorts all the time, even in winter. He is an eccentric, like me. Like all of us. But I am not single. I am always in love.

I love to be in love. I write this for one of the girls I love.

When I Fall

At the first syllable of her voice
I fall
As if I'm left without a choice
When she calls
Whatever for
I have yet to know
For what reason
She has walked through my heart's door
When I fall
All I can do is hope
That she'll be there
When I land
Waiting for me
With her hand
What we feel
For each other
Will reveal
Only time will tell
Only time will heal
Love should be spent
Every day as if it is its last
Not a day in the future
Nor a day in the past.

Girls and then women I love, from grade one to age twenty-six:

Monika.
Jen.
Claire.
Sabah.
Shabnam.
Emma.
Maria. (Once after visiting her in Collingwood my dad asks me how it was. "Blessed and stressed," I say.)
Wynee. (Who laughs and cries without restraint, and wears perfume and makeup, and loves Korean food as much as me. I eat with her at Seoul on Bloor Street. I tell my dad, "It was the bib of bops." And on the phone to my girlfriend I say, "Wynee Love, you can have all my handsomeness!" And she giggles and giggles.)

I write so many poems for all of my beloveds. But very few of these poems do I actually give to them.

I am in Guelph with my dad and Luisa to give a keynote speech at a fundraiser for Prader-Willi Syndrome research. It is May, 2018. Luisa helps me set up my jewellery display. The idea is I give the speech and then sell lots of jewellery. Good business marketing technique! Luisa also cooks delicious food and teaches me to cook, and to ALWAYS smell the spices and herbs before putting them in. I even cooked chicken parmesan for Wynee and me. And Luisa gives good shoulder rubs whenever I ask her. She and my dad put the earrings on my birdcage display, which is hard to do unless you have good fine motor skills. Ryan, the organizer, introduces me and cries a little because he says I am his inspiration. He and his wife have two daughters, one with Prader-Willi Syndrome and the other with Down Syndrome. I'm glad they will hear this speech, which I worked hard on. It is for them, and all of my friends with all of their syndromes, and everyone in the world who is different. Luisa and my dad are sitting right in front of me, just behind a buffet table I plan to explore after my speech. I step up to the podium and begin.

Hello Everyone! Before I begin, I would like to thank Ryan Kelly and anyone else who helped organize this event for inviting me to talk about my personal experience with a disability. I would also like to thank everyone for coming out and supporting this cause!

My name is Jacob Zavitz. I am twenty-six years young (I say years young, because I too like to flatter myself and ignore how old I really am!). I am an unadulterated adult who has never committed adultery. I am also a poet, photographer, a jeweller, and I work for Toronto Police Services as a crossing guard!

I have come to this event today to talk about my first-hand experience living as an individual with a disability. I was diagnosed when I was four years old. My parents didn't understand much about what I had at the time and didn't try to explain to me what I was going through or why my life was noticeably different from others' until I reached the age of eight years old.

By the time I was twelve, I had attended many conferences and on occasion heard the doctors speak about my disability. They used a lot of medical terms which I didn't understand, and found boring. This is what I heard:

Symptoms of Prader-Willi Syndrome are and not limited to blah blah blah Hyper Phagia blah blah blah. Prader-Willi Syndrome is caused by blah blah blah lack of or multiple chromosome WTF's blah blah blah.

I would now like to take this opportunity to explain in the simplest words and in the form of a poem by twelve-year-old Jacob Zavitz about his perception of what Prader Blah Blah Blah Syndrome is:

Stumbling Through Hunger

Stumbling through hunger,
Looking for food,
Walking through hallways
Due to a feeling
That you need to eat,
Led off your feet,
To start your seek,
Stomach grumbling,
Fuel gauge busted,
Your memory rusted,
Not remembering what you ate,
Knowing you're out of date,
With your unknown weight,
Nervous about a lot of things.
And worried,
Ashamed of your problems
Makes it hard to talk about things

Having no control over
Your temptations.
You cannot stop.
It cannot end.

When I was in elementary school grade 1-6, I ate the food my
parents packed for me and ate the food other parents packed
for their kids. The lunch boxes were in bins outside of the
classroom. With very little supervision available for kids with
disabilities at the time (mid-2000's) I would select an item from
various lunch boxes (to avoid suspicion) therefore providing
for myself another lunch to eat. My favourite lunch items were:
Hong Guen's Korean red bean and walnut cakes, Brien Diep's
Chinese hot dog in a sticky bun, Iouri's European delights. This
is how I became a multiculturally educated individual!

In middle school, lunch boxes and bins were extinct, so I decided
to pay other students to deliver pizza to me, and I would store it all
in my locker, and take several (cough*cough*) washroom breaks.

The hardest challenges of my life started when I attended George
Brown College for a goldsmithing education. I learned forms of
goldsmithing, hand fabrication, and model-making out of wax.
However, I did not have any support from anyone for the first
three years, and bought extra food every day, gained lots of
weight, and carried my life's stresses on my broad fat shoulders.
I was happy to have been accepted into college, and have the
opportunity to learn something cool, and was proud of myself
for it. However, having an eating disorder and being constantly
hungry, and not having support, I had to eventually swallow my
pride and ask for help. My family hired a support worker, and
despite our differences at times, having support helped me feel
more comfortable in the last two years of my semi-independent
college life.

I am now an adult. My challenges haven't really changed day to day
from when I was younger. However my quality of life has become

greater because of my ability to cope with or find solutions to reduce my day-to-day challenges by making better decisions.

I still have an eating disorder. I still have hyperphagia, and I still break into the forbidden fridge at home on occasion.

You may be wondering after what I just finished saying, how could my quality of life have improved if such challenges re-occur?

Well, as an adult I have learned to embrace my disability rather than ignore it. I have learned to ask for help rather than to become sicker from my secrets.

I have learned that, although I have a disability, I am able to do many things and succeed at them.

I am not Prader-Willi Syndrome but have Prader-Willi Syndrome. Living with a disability doesn't define who I am because I am who defines who I am.

I am a crossing guard for Toronto Police Services.
I am a jewellery designer.
I am a photographer.
I am a fisherman.
I have Prader-Willi Syndrome.
I AM Jacob Zavitz!

(And at this line everyone starts clapping and I see people crying and I see my dad and Luisa smiling so proudly and I look at the crowd and feel so much joy that I improvise something that wasn't in the speech. I pretend to read my script and I say: "'Break for applause' was actually built into the script ..." And then there is a great roar of laughter and I've never heard such laughing at something I've said, and I understand how important it is to the people in front of me who are parents and grandparents of people with disabilities to hear someone like me being so funny.)

I will start to close my keynote by offering a few pieces of advice and mentioning a couple of other things.

Don't think about what doctors say your child can't or is unable to do. Instead, wait and be patient and you will discover what your child is capable of doing.

Lock your fridge and pantry early in your child's life, so as they grow up it will feel normal.

If you plan to go out to a restaurant as a family, look at the menu at home with your child and agree ahead of time on what they will order.

Compliment your child whenever you feel they have done something they should be proud of.

The last couple of things I would like to mention are:

I have donated a pearl necklace to the auction. For those interested, you should bid on it, because adrenaline is good for you. For those of you with questions, come on over to my jewellery table, and I will answer any of your questions with the purchase of any jewellery item. For those who do not have questions, come to my table anyway and purchase a piece of jewellery. It will help me buy my next fishing rod, camera body, lens, or help pay my Visa bill.

Thank you!

And they all stand up and clap and I am crying a little bit from all of this love and Luisa is there with a hug and we go to my table and by the end of the night I sell $1,000 worth of necklaces and earrings.

My names:

Cobi.

Jakeronamus. That's from Grandpa Jack.

Jakespeare, when I do spoken word.

Rymedikulous, another one of my poet names, which Clifton Joseph still remembers and uses when he sees me.

Blues Jake, from when Oliver Schroer and Soozi Schlanger play music with me.

Kid. That's from my big brother.

Jacob Evan, which has my middle name, which comes from a poetry teacher named Evan Pike who my mom had in high school. When it's time for bed my dad calls out from the top of the stairs, "Jacob Evan Yashinsky-Zavitz, are you ready for your foot rub?" Sometimes it is: "Mister Yashinsky-Zavitz." He gives me a foot rub at night. My feet get so sore from all the walking I do for my job.

Da Baby. That's what I call myself when I'm very young and my parents ask me what my name is, and even though I know my name is "Jacob," I tease them by saying, "Da Baby," and they laugh and say it sounds like I'm a Chicago gangster.

I am in Montreal with my dad and my best friend, Effie. It is the hottest day in a hundred years. Effie and I have done so many things: watching the Canada Day fireworks in the Old City and taking photos, so many photos. I get a shot of the fireworks exploding behind the giant Ferris wheel. I like the way the Ferris wheel becomes part of the explosion.

Later we go for beers and dessert. We have been riding the bus, taking photos, eating poutine and chocolate cake. Before we leave the city, we go up to Mont Royal and Effie and I take more photos. We are hot. And happy. It is so hot that I ask a French gardener who is spraying his hose on the plants at the Kondiaronk Belvedere that looks over the city to spray me too. Effie is taking pictures. My dad is laughing. He says, "You are probably the only person in the history of Montreal who has ever done such a thing!" And I think: I have done so many things where I am the only person who has ever done such things.

And then we begin our drive home.

We stop at a tackle store on the outskirts of Montreal, which I had noticed on the way into the city two days before. I buy new lures for walleye. We are going fishing the day after we get home. I've never caught a walleye, just my brother did once, and he doesn't know anything about fishing, and I'm the one with all the top-end gear. I have caught bass and pike and even a muskie, but never a walleye. The lures are in the back of our Ford Escape, along with our camera equipment.

My dad is driving and Effie is in the back seat. We pull out on to the highway. I am eating a Cuban sandwich in the hot car. Even with the air conditioning on, the car is hot. My dad got my sandwich in the Plateau before he packed the car for our drive home. I finish my delicious sandwich and fall asleep.

I wake up as we are crashing and I can't breathe anymore, and I hear my dad saying that Effie is okay, and the ambulance is coming soon, and that he's so sorry he fell asleep, and I begin my journey away from the 401 and from that hot day and from the broken car and from my crying father and from my best friend. But then the paramedics come and even though I can't see anymore, I want to stay awhile yet, and I do, and I get to hear my brother's voice and my mother's voice and feel their tears on my face even though I can't tell them how much I love them, or even say anything at all.

The car stops rolling.

I am so scared.

I pee myself.

I can't breathe.

I ask my dad, "Where is the ambulance?"

It is so hot in the car.

The smell of smashed metal.

Effie is okay in the back seat.

My dad is screaming and holding me.

"It is on its way, sweetheart," he says.

"Just hang in there. Please. PLEASE!"

Then I stop feeling the heat.

There is no pain.

I hear a siren.

I can't breathe.

I don't want to die.

I'm almost twenty-seven years old.

Why isn't the ambulance here?

Why did my father crash?

I am so scared.

I want my mother.

I am sliding down the waterslide at Piccininni pool—my dad calls it "pinch-your-weenie"—and my Grandpa Jack is at the bottom to catch me as I squeal and splash into the water. I am three years old.

This is like that, happening so fast, like a fast slide, no breath, no breath, and I am saying to my dad, "Am I dying?" and he is screaming something and yelling, "Please! Please!" and then I begin to leave and my grandpa is there catching me, just like when I am three years old coming down the slide.

But I decide to stay because I want so much to hear my brother's voice again, and my mother's voice again, and my dad's voice not screaming. So I am staying to listen to their voices, even though I am already near my grandpa's open arms.

My brother cries on my chest in the intensive care unit. I'm far, far away, almost without my body, almost disconnected from life support. But safe, listening to him say he loves me.

The first time he cried just for me was in my crazy time, when I became psychotic. I am in my early twenties and I am standing at St. Clair West and Christie Street in front of World Class Bakers and my support worker is with me but I can barely walk or talk and she calls my dad in a panic and he calls my brother, and my big brother comes charging up Christie Street hill at full speed and hugs me tight so tight and cries as he holds me and asks me to get treatment because he needs me to be healthy again. And I am so sick, but I feel his hot tears soaking into my shirt, and I think, somehow very deep inside, that if my big, tough brother needs me so much then I will try to get better, and will try to be a good man and a good son and a good brother. He is tough and rough and cool and here he is holding me and crying and crying and that makes a window in my wrecked mind and I say "Yes." And I go to the psychiatric hospital, and I get treatment, and I quit drugs, and my mind comes back to me, and I get better. I even begin working for the Toronto Police Services as a crossing guard, where you have to be wide awake all the time to keep the children safe. And I make a best friend named Effie. And I become a photographer. And I play backgammon with Luisa and even with my brother. And he and I trash-talk each other, which is the best thing ever. And his tears melt an opening, and my life becomes good and beautiful and full of responsibility and love.

And now he is crying again, and I feel his tears though I can't speak, and he is asking me not to die. But I am going to leave soon because I was hurt too badly in the accident. And even as I am leaving I can feel his tears are there on my cheek and on my chest, and I feel safe and so loved because there is nothing as good as being loved by a brother as cool and tough as my big brother.

I am fishing on Roddick Lake, going further and further. I go around the point and through the narrows and all the way across the other part of the lake to the bay where a creek comes in. It takes a long time to get there, but I always wanted to fish around that creek. My mom is back at the cottage and my dad is still back home in the city. I start going up the creek and get stuck. I can't get the kayak free. I can't reach my mom because there's no reception. I have no idea how to get home, except back across the lake. So I leave the kayak and walk up through a farmer's field. I come to the farmhouse and explain that I'm lost. I don't speak French and they don't speak English but they let me use their phone and luckily Mom picks up. She figures out where I am and drives over to get me. Then when my dad comes, we go back and load the kayak on top of the car.

Another time I'm out on the lake and don't see that behind me the thunderclouds are building and building, getting darker and darker. When I finally look behind me, I see the storm coming. I pedal full steam ahead and keep close to the shore and get back to the cottage just as the lightning tears the sky open and the whitecaps come up on the lake. My mom is waiting on the dock. She gives me a big, wet hug and we drag the boat up on the sand and go inside.

My dad and I are taking a hike up the hill at the cottage. I am seven or so, and pretty big because I have Prader-Willi Syndrome. We get lost trying to come down the hillside and wind up in a bushy, mucky, swampy part of the forest. I am so tired and pretty worried. My dad picks me up and carries me, even though I am big, and we find the trail and get home, and I tell my mom about getting lost. We never go up the hill again because it is so easy to get lost on the way down.

And I wonder how someone can love you so much and still do something that causes you harm, like falling asleep while driving us home from Montreal. And I carry my father's cries in the wrecked car, and I also carry his love. And I carry everything, all my loves, all my gifts. And then it is no longer possible to carry anything, and I become the one who is being carried, like when we get lost in the swamp.

I'm standing on the dock butt naked. I'm four years old. I yell, "O Canada!" and jump in. My mom and dad are already in the water. They are laughing. Then for all my life my mom tells me how my little white *tuches* glimmered in the emerald-green water as I dive and dive and dive like a baby dolphin.

And one day my dad and I are swimming at the Jewish Community Centre pool with Ron Evans, our Indigenous friend. I am twelve or so. I keep swimming around Ron, teasing him. He says, "If you keep doing that I'm going to hold you underwater so long bubbles will come out of your ass." I laugh and laugh, diving down and then popping back up to laugh some more.

Then I'm standing on another dock on another lake where I've come with my dad to do some fishing. I'm twenty-five. My dad is already in the water. He just dives in, but I take after my mother and I get in very slowly. My dad sometimes does a haka on the deck to get ready to dive in. He tells me a haka is what the Maori warriors do in New Zealand before a battle. My dad jumps up and down on the dock and yells, "HAKA! HAKA! HAKA!" He says I should try it. One day I tell him: "You should go haka yourself!" We laugh. The water is cold in Crow Lake that summer. It takes me a long time to get up the courage to jump, but then I say, "You can't unjump a jump!" and I jump in. We are laughing. We say that whenever we have to decide something important: "You can't unjump a jump."

We are swimming to the raft. We go there every summer to stay in Frans' cottage. The other people on the lake call us "*les anglais fous*" because we swim even if the lake is cold and rough. When we get to the raft, I climb out while my mom and dad tread water or swim around the raft. Then I jump in and we all swim together past the big rock that marks halfway to the cottage. If I get tired, I rest on my dad's foam noodle. If a boat is coming near, we splash around until we see them change course. I am eight and we are swimming as a speedboat comes towards us. I tell my dad, "Holy, man, hold up your noodle!" The boat veers aside. At home, a snack and hot shower.

Leaving is like jumping off the raft and landing in a whole other lake than the one I had climbed out of. And instead of my mom and dad, there are both of my grandpas, Jack and Jim, waiting for me. And many, many others.

Your voices are becoming distant. Beeping of monitors, like when I was born in the neonatal intensive care unit. My brother's face, his voice, his hot tears on my face. The tears flow with me slow time, no hurry now. My sweet brother. His rough voice. His smell. The way he says I'm the Fresh Prince of St. Clair. The way he says, "Hey kid." He is talking to our mom and dad. He is telling little stories about me. And he says that whenever he blew out the candles on his birthday cake growing up, he always gave his wish to me. His secret wish, that you can't say out loud. My brother. My brother's voice. My brother's birthday wishes.

It is the eighth day in the trauma centre.

I must leave now.

I am carrying all of your voices, all my loves.

A giant turtle is coming towards me

And picking me up.

A turtle as old as the earth.

She is the earth.

Grandmother Earth.

And she picks me up gently

And we begin to walk away

Very,

Very,

Very,

Very,

Slowly,

And it is quiet

And I am not afraid anymore

And I become part of Her

As we move slowly, even slower than my St. Clair saunter,

Slower than time,

Slowly moving away,

Leaving.

I am leaving you. I am in my Hobie Pro Angler heading across a really big lake, maybe Roddick but much, much bigger, and there is a morning mist and I am gliding towards the far shore and my grandfathers are waiting for me and I want to look back, and I do look back, but all I see is the mist behind me and my home shore gone.

At my funeral my dad tosses his brown fedora on the coffin as everyone takes turns shovelling dirt and crying. Wynee cries wild grief at the graveside, but I am so far away. Kimchee, my beloved. Bibimbap.

When they hear the news, they put up white paper hearts in the trees at the Winona and Benson intersection. They love me, the kids and the parents and the woman who has mental health problems but always walks her therapy dog when I am on shift because I am always kind to her, and the grade six boy with the big afro who I tease and who says, "My hair is bigger than your future!" and the middle schoolers who try to cross without waiting for me to stop traffic, and who laugh when I shout, "hashtag WE KNOW BETTER!" and the mother who lives up the street and lets her grade four girl walk by herself as soon as she sees me waiting for her, and my old teachers and daycare staff from when I went to McMurrich P.S., and Winona Middle School, and Sprouts Daycare, and everyone who knew me from when I was young and they are all so proud that I became a good man, and that I keep the children safe, and the mother's tears holding her toddler after I save her life.

How I am still with you.

Walking on St. Clair.

With Jewelz when she flops on her back and asks to have her tummy scratched.

In the smell of rotis from Albert's Real Jamaican at Vaughan and St. Clair.

In rainbows.

In red-tailed hawks.

In the otter on Leslie Spit.

In cardinals.

In Monarch butterflies.

In the whales my brother sees in the Pacific Ocean.

In dreams.

I carry you all, meals, kisses, injera from the Ethiopian restaurant, doubles from Gerry's, rotis from Albert's, Dutch Dreams ice cream double scoop with topping, my mom's big hugs, my brother's voice, the *shvitz* at the Jewish Community Centre, my kids crossing at Winona and Benson, *How I Met Your Mother*, *NCIS* and watching all the episodes of all the seasons with my beautiful mother, the standing ovation after my speech, my vape, bass, pike, my one muskie, the click of my Nikon shutter, Effie's laugh, Effie saying, "Oh my GOD!" the day we met, Appleton's rum at games nights, my dad's foot rubs at night, Luisa sauntering beside me instead of hurrying ahead like the others, my support workers, rods, reels, fedoras, pearls, semi-precious gemstones, my RRSP, my grandparents, Mishigas the border collie, Jewelz our mutt who I chose and named, love, love, Wynee's smile when we pick her up from her group home, her bare breasts, her perfume, *The Sopranos*, fishing with my dad and calling out "FISH ON!", laughing when Natty teases me, calculating my jewellery profits, the farmers' market at the Barns on Saturday morning, all of my eccentrics on St. Clair West, love and love, Chez Jose on the Plateau in Montreal, New York, Holland, Grandpa Jack's potage, singing JOLENE JOLENE JOLENE JOLENE with the neighbours, singing along with Janis Joplin with the windows rolled down and "TAKE IT! Take another little piece of my heart ...", Bernard's funny green elf slippers, the time I went outside at a seder so I could knock on the door as Elijah the Prophet, kombucha after a workout, showing Bernard my stuff, pedalling my Hobie Pro Angler, fishing with my wacky-rigged Sankos, swapping dirty jokes with my dad, and LamborGHINI!, and reading Jewish jokes in the bathroom, the Feast of the Red Bean when my dad's oldest friends come and we sing and eat all night long, hip hop, love, every morning having espresso at Krave on my way to the intersection, my mom's grin, my cool brother, love, Jewelz licking my face when I cry or pretty much anytime, Kensington Market, my fur coats, my birdcage display full of earrings, my Cuban sandwich in the car on our drive back from Montreal and eating it on the 401 and telling my dad, "This is delicious!" and feeling full, and keeping my children safe with my stop sign and my whistle and my strong arms held out to keep the traffic under control, and seeing them all coming towards me to cross Winona and Benson on their way to school, my intersection, being responsible, being sane, being a man, all of my children, safe because I am here and will protect them, and I blow my whistle and I blow my whistle and I blow my whistle, and I am full.

A Note for Grieving Parents

When Jacob's brother Nathaniel spoke at the funeral, he said that love continues to exist in the world even though his little brother is gone. Somehow, love remains. There are many loves, sensed even in the ruins and depths of grief. The love of family and close friends as you rebuild your shattered lives together. The love for the one who died. The love for all of your spirit-people, gone before you to wherever souls go. The love of your memories as the years pass and shock abates and you slowly find a voice to recollect and share them. The love imbuing the little rituals of daily life: walking my son's dog (who, years later, keeps looking for her real owner) in the ravine, going for a swim in the neighbourhood pool, having an espresso at the same café where we would go every morning. The steadfast love and wisdom of our oldest son. Most of all, sensing the immense, unshakeable love Jacob beamed so radiantly on those who loved him. All of these loves hold us and bind us to this world and remind us why we must keep living and loving.

Acknowledgments

Endless thanks to:

Karen Haughian and the team at Signature Editions.

Friends and family who read and/or listened to this book as it evolved: Nina Abdelmessih, Pramila Aggarwal, Einya Artzi, Effie Biliris, Rebecca Boroson, John Brady, Jose Brown, Annemarie Cabri, Ted Chamberlin, Mark Comstock, Mary Anne Cree, Ray de Breyne, Ron Evans, Jonathan Fox, Jaron Freeman-Fox, Iris Gershon, Nadien Godkewitsch, Cecilia Green, Jonathan Hellmann, Lo Humeniuk, Brian Katz, Bernard Kelly, Hans Kleipool, Nathan Lawrie, Barbara Lazar, Gunilla Likwornik, Charmaine Lurch, Christine Malec, Cathy Mallove, Moyo Mutamba, Michael Pestel, Itah Sadu, Carmen Schifellite, Luisa Sousa, Larissa Swenarchuk, Anna Walker, Mark Yashinsky, Suzanne Yashinsky, Ellen Yeomans.

Gabi Caruso, for painting and giving us the wonderful portrait of Jacob, and her permission to use it on the cover.

The Ontario Prader-Willi Syndrome Association, for all of the love and support you bring PWS families.

Carol Zavitz, for being the best of mothers to Natty and Jacob.

Natty Zavitz for suggesting these stories about his little brother be shared, and for being, with Stephanie Hooker and Isha Jasmine Yashinsky-Zavitz, my light-bringers in the darkest times.

Photo Credits

Page 70, "tough-guy Jacob" by Daniel Kennedy

Page 96, Toronto Storytelling Festival poster image by Belinda Ageda

Page 125, Natty, Dan and Jacob by Kat Rizza

Page 159, Dan and Jacob by Andrew Fishman

Pages 83, 100, 106, 112, 114, 120, 136 by Jacob Yashinsky-Zavitz

Pages 17, 31, 36, 40, 45, 88, 93, 116, Yashinsky-Zavitz family

Dan Yashinsky

Dan co-founded the Toronto Storytelling Festival, the Storytellers School of Toronto and the 1001 Friday Nights of Storytelling. He has been a storyteller-in-residence at Queen's University, Toronto Public Library, The Stop Community Food Centre, Storytelling Toronto, UNICEF Canada and Baycrest Health Sciences, working in psychiatry, palliative care, and in the dementia program. Dan has performed at festivals in Israel, Sweden, Norway, Holland, England, Wales, England, Germany, Brazil, Austria, France, the U.S., Singapore, and Ireland, as well as all across Canada.

Dan's previous books include *Suddenly They Heard Footsteps* (Knopf Canada), *Swimming with Chaucer—A Storyteller's Logbook* (Insomniac Press), and *Tales for an Unknown City* (McGill-Queen's University Press). He also has a children's book, *The Golden Apples*, forthcoming with Running the Goat Books & Broadsides.

Eco-Audit
Printing this book using Rolland Enviro100 Book
instead of virgin fibres paper saved the following resources:

Trees	Water	Air Emissions
3	1,000 L	180 kg